The Song of Irrelevance
Meditation of what you are

Karl Renz

Edited By
Manjit Achhra

The Song of Irrelevance
Meditation of what you are

Karl Renz

Edited By
Manjit Achhra

A Division of Maoli Media Private Limited

*This dance of consciousness,
trying to find a perfect match with itself, will never stop.*

*This inquiry is an infinite game.
It will always dance with itself and look for a perfect dancer,
a perfect dance, a perfect harmony.*

KARL RENZ

The Song of Irrelevance

Copyright © 2013 Karl Renz

First Edition: January 2013

PUBLISHED BY
ZEN PUBLICATIONS
A Division of Maoli Media Private Limited
60, Juhu Supreme Shopping Centre,
Gulmohar Cross Road No. 9, JVPD Scheme,
Juhu, Mumbai 400 049. India.
Tel: +91 9022208074
eMail: info@zenpublications.com
Website: www.zenpublications.com

Book Design: Red Sky Designs, Mumbai
Cover Image: Detail of a painting by Karl Renz

ISBN 978-93-82788-02-7

All rights reserved. No part of this book may be reproduced or transmitted in any form or by any means, electronic or mechanical, including photocopying, recording, or by any information storage and retrieval system without written permission from the author or his agents, except for the inclusion of brief quotations in a review.

Contents

Acknowledgement	9
The end of the end	11
See you again - next time	43
When you are - you are shit	73
Even the understanding 'everything is consciousness' - is bullshit	103
Even oneness is fascism because it claims to be better than separation	140
I Am That - What is stupidity itself	165
Even saying that there is nothing to find, is a goal on the way	195

Other Books by Karl Renz

- A Little Bit Of Nothingness
  81 Observations On The Unnamable
- Heaven and Hell
- Am I - I Am
- May It Be As It Is
  The Embrace of Helplessness
- If You Wake Up, Don't Take It Personally
  Dialogues in the Presence of Arunachala
- The Myth of Enlightenment
  Seeing Through the Illusion of Separation

Other Books by Zen Publications

- Redemption Stories: Unwasted Pain
- A Duet of One
- Pursue 'Happiness' And Get Enlightened
- Pointers From Ramana Maharshi
- Enlightened Living
- A Buddha's Babble
- A Personal Religion Of Your Own
- The Essence of The Ashtavakra Gita
- The Relationship Between 'I' And 'Me'
- Seeking Enlightenment – Why ?
- Nuggets of Wisdom
- Confusion No More
- Guru Pournima
- Advaita and the Buddha
- It So Happened That... The Unique Teaching of Ramesh S. Balsekar
- Sin and Guilt: Monstrosity of Mind
- The Infamous Ego
- Who Cares?!
- The Essence of the Bhagavad Gita
- Your Head in the Tiger's Mouth
- Consciousness Writes
- Consciousness Speaks
- The Bhagavad Gita – A Selection

ACKNOWLEDGEMENT

𝒯he Publishers wish to thank
Sanjay Inamdar, Hemant Nadkarni and Amrita Hinduja
for their invaluable help in making this book possible.

Karl Renz

The End of the End

Q: When we woke you up right now, what happened to your perception? You heard us waking up, somebody called Karl and then immediately everything was there or...

K: It was already there.

Q: When you are in deep sleep, do you actually perceive it?

K: I am not in deep sleep.

Q: In deep-deep sleep?

K: There is no one in deep-deep sleep, there is no one here.

Q: But there is a perception, right?

K: Perception is always!

Q: And the perception of Karl?

K: What about the perceived Karl?

Q: What happened when we woke you up?

K: Nothing happened. What should happen?

Q: I just want to know what happens with your personal perception?

K: There is no personal perception.

Q: That's all I know, I just know my personal perception...

K: You have no personal perception!

Q: But is there an experience of personal perception?

K: No.

Q: Then what I'm experiencing now?

K: You are experiencing Yorden, but that is not a personal perception. That is a personal experience and not a personal perception.

Q: But the perception feels very personal...

K: The perception never feels anything. You cannot feel perception. Don't claim something you cannot do. What bullshit is that?

Q: We are just playing with words...

K: We are not playing with words, you cannot experience perception. Whatever can be experienced is not perception.

Q: I don't know...

K: I know that you don't know.

Q: To me, it seems like I experience perception. If I hit my hand...

K: That is not perception, that's an experience.

Q: But where is the perception then?

K: It is always prior to what you experience.

Q: But in experience there must be perception...

K: There is perception but it is not perceived. Perception can never be perceived otherwise there would be two perceptions. Which perception is perceiving which perception?

Q: Then you're talking about something else that I normally experience and see...

K: You talk about experiences but not about perception.

Q: I talk about that what I perceive...

K: But that is not perception. The seer is already perceived but the perception, that is perceiving the perceiver, can never be perceived.

Q: These are just words. Can you show it to me?

K: What?

Q: But how can I see it?

K: I just said it you cannot see it. What bullshit are you talking about?

[Crow caws]

K: Shut up!

[Crow continues cawing]

Q [Another visitor]: There is no one who cares for your shut up...

K: Look at him. He is Mr. Sadhu on the run. Do you think that's the only bird that doesn't listen to me? All these birds, [pointing to visitors] they never listen. [Laughter]

Q [Another visitor]: But can one listen to you?

K: No!

Q: Can one understand something?

K: No! Otherwise I would kill them right away. If there would be some 'one' here who would understand or would-not understand, I would kill them right away.

Q [Another visitor]: Could or would-not? [Laughter]

K: Both is impossible! If there could be one who could [understand], then he claims that he wouldn't.

Q [Another visitor]: But how would you kill him?

K: I would show him how to fly!

Q [Another visitor]: If I say I'm dying or afraid of death, you say there is nobody dying. So how can you kill somebody?

K: That is what I just said. You don't listen! He tries to be clever and never listens...

Q: I'm not clever.

K: I'm not clever? [Laughing] Now he is very clever. Who claims that he is not clever? The one who is really clever. Mr. Cleverly!

Q [Another visitor]: If everything is perception, can there be a shift in perception?

K: Of course!

Q: Can it be explained? The shift in perception?

K: It can be explained, but doesn't mean that you would understand it.

Q: For what will this explanation then be good?

K: For nothing! That's the beauty of it. No one needs it.

Q: So I just play with words?

K: If you could play with words, it would be permanent fun. But now the words play with you.

Q [Another visitor]: What about the shift from understanding to not understanding anything anymore?

K: No. That cannot happen. Understanding is permanent.

Q: Like perception?

K: Like perception.

Q: Is there no understanding in understanding?

K: There is understanding but no 'one' who understands.

Q: But no 'one' who understands anything...

K: It doesn't matter!

Q: Perception is always, understanding is always...

K: Whatever is, is always...

Q: And there is no one in it, no one having it, no one being it...

K: There is not even 'no one'.

Q: I'm trying to understand again and again and it's hopeless. As a phantom, I cannot understand what you are talking about. I cannot! It's impossible!

K: Now you understand that you cannot understand, but the understanding is there. Was there any moment there was no understanding?

Q: No...

K: So there's always understanding and there's always knowledge. Even if you claim not to know, there is knowledge. But inspite of one who knows or doesn't know, there is knowledge. That's what I always point to and there is always perception inspite of a presence of a perceiver or absence of a perceiver. I don't say anything else.

So you may say that what is your nature, is with and without one who is 'experienced'. So saying that there is no one, is still one too many and it doesn't work. You are with and without.

Q: This movement that you want to get somewhere or you want to get something like enlightenment or the dissolution of the search is totally non-sense. It's hopeless...

K: That's the beauty of it.

Q: I'm fed up with it...

K: Even that is beautiful. You are playing 'fed-up' looking for yourself. For how long? And then you start again and even by being fed-up, you look for yourself because you think that maybe by being fed-up, you find something.

Q: So...

K: Keep looking. You cannot otherwise. When the seer wakes up, the looking happens for That what is the seer. You cannot avoid it. Even trying not to look is looking for yourself. So what is the advantage of not looking? Or what is the disadvantage of looking?

Q: It's all too much effort...

K: For who? For bloody who?

Q: For the phantom...

K: The phantom never did anything and what-you-are is inexhaustible. even the phantom is inexhaustible because when you-are, the phantom-is – energy itself. How can you exhaust energy? But you try and you never succeed.

So you look and be happy. Enjoy the looking, enjoy the seeking and enjoy that you cannot find in seeking, enjoy the not finding, but you can never stop looking.

Q: Will it never stop?

K: It never started. How can that stop what never started? Try to find the beginning. The entire scientific world looks for the big bang and they could not find it. They just claim something, that comes close to something, but it's all fiction.

Q: That's already the Self looking for the Self?

K: Absolutely! What is the scientific world? It's the Self looking for the Self. You think you are the only seeker? The whole consciousness playing a scientific bullshit – They are looking for what is 'Truth'. It cannot be found, but they keep looking. They cannot stop it. Even by trying not to look, they expect something by not looking.

Q: But isn't a Sage the one that stops?

K: No! A Sage simply enjoys looking, without expectation of finding. That is the difference between the one who is looking and expecting to find and one who is looking without expectation to find. That is what makes the Sage, but in nature they're not different.

So that is why it's said that *jñani* is the one who enjoys to the maximum that the *jñani* cannot be found, but it is still looking and enjoying the not finding. You become a little one who expects that by your action or looking you can find yourself – that makes you exhaustible and tired already.

So because you look for a happy end, you are exhausted already. The *jñani* may know that there was no beginning and never expect anything to end – not even himself you are someone who started and will end someday. So you are something what can be exhausted, with that you're already tired.

What are we doing here? I'm just pointing to the inexhaustible nature of what-you-are. And by being it, you are the inexhaustible energy which is still looking for itself but not expecting to find it. Because this is the way you realize yourself. Realizing yourself as a seeker, seeking that what is the seeker – infinitely. It never started and will never end, as you never started and will never end.

So when I say you better be That what-you-cannot-not-be, it's That what is the energy of the seeker, the energy of the seeking and the energy of what is being sought. That can never be exhausted and is never tired. That you can call the absolute seer which is in it's nature, a perception and perception can never be tired by anything and is never more or less.

That's the quality of what-you-are. The quality which is never more or less. There is no quantity of more or less experiencing. So be the quality and not some bullshit quantity of shit and only shit can be exhausted.

Q [Another visitor]: Is it true that each individual search or expression is different? Like a fingerprint...

K: Every experience is unique. Every aspect of realization is unique. There is no second to That. Even in That, there is no second. Unicity is all there is. It's like a flake of snow, you cannot find a second one which is same. Each moment is absolutely unique, there is no twin.

Q: The tricky thing that I find with spiritual teachers is that there is a common understanding, that people think that this way is the right way to go about, by meditating or by understanding or beingness and you smash it all the time. So there is no way even to draw a line. In the spiritual world there is pressure to perform or do or act in a particular way otherwise you are not good enough...

K: It's like you are always in a school, you have to perform as the teacher wants you. That's why it's called the *dharma*-keeper who keeps the teachings alive and there is a difference between what is the right way and the wrong way. All that is needed by those religions. Then you need *shakti* from your master and you're always in this master-disciple relationship and you are never good enough in that way – as much as you try. In my case, it didn't even start to be in any spiritual way. Because for me there is no question of how far you are or how advanced you are. Because there was never anyone who was ever advanced in anything.

So I'm looking in to your nature and That is always quality itself and the rest is fiction anyway and to That – no way leads. That is the absolute no-way of Buddha. No way! What ever is in the way is a phantom and the phantom can only be advanced or disadvanced.

Q [Another visitor]: Yesterday you said to me that I am like a baby and that sounded not advanced...

K: Be happy when I call you a baby, that you never learned anything. Because your nature never needs to learn anything. You are like a baby. Take it as a compliment and not be offended by it. I make a compliment and she gets offended, it's absolutely amazing.

Q [Another visitor]: It didn't sound like a compliment yesterday...

K: Not for you because for the one who thinks he knows something, it's not a compliment to be called as a baby. For sure you are not, because you are not a baby. You are half grown up. [Laughter]

Q [Another visitor]: I don't believe you, about the compliment...

K: I always make compliments. You are just not used to compliments.

Q: Especially from you...

K: I'm permanently making compliments to That what I Am. I Am an absolute compliment.

Q [Another visitor]: Would you say there is a last understanding which doesn't need to be understood?

K: No.

Q: The Absolute knowing doesn't need knowing and not-knowing, but still there must be somebody...

K: Even knowing doesn't need anyone to know That.

Q: Yes...

K: But you just said the opposite.

Q: You experience this non-happening or happening. So you have to have it...

K: How many times did I talk to you about this split second?

Q: I know it theoretically, but again 'who'?

K: There is no 'who' in it, that is the whole point of the split second because without the second there is no one.

Q: But it has to be something...

K: What something?

Q [Another visitor]: Yesterday you talked about the breaking of the heart knot...

K: The breaking of the heart knot is the end of the love affair with yourself, in a relative way.

Q: So there is an end...

K: Yeah, there was a beginning and that can end. It begins like your body started and it ends.

Q: But then the heart knot can start again?

K: Yeah, with something else – Of course. If 'your' heart knot breaks, there are too many 'others' who have a heart knot. Otherwise if it would break for someone, it should break for everyone – instantly.

Q: So there's actually no heart knot breaking?

K: There is a heart knot breaking but it's of a relative, personal – 'My bloody heart knot broke'. [Laughter] If the Self has to realize itself to be itself, then by Jesus, Ramana or anyone of them, the Self should have been realized. Then why does it still look for itself? Now in seven billion people, the Self is looking for the Self or happiness. Why should it still look for happiness when it realized that it cannot be happy by any phenomenal experience by all those Sages, by all those realized ones.

Nothing happens by all those bloody realizations.

Q: But all these guys you talked about, does it happen to them? Or nothing happens?

K: Even Ramana said that there was never any one who was unrealized and that's the split second. How can that what was never unrealized – realize?

Q: That's what he constantly says when everyone talks about self-realization, he says 'What Self is not realized? Self is realization'. It's not like something that happens...

K: Was the Self at any moment not realized? This is splitting the second. This is an absolute knowledge That you are never-never in a way. That what-you-are is never-never. It's not like in one moment you are not realized and in the next moment you are realized.

Q: So actually there's no split second...

K: There are many split seconds. There's only the split second. There was never anything else other than split second.

Q: I understand...

K: You see it's possible to understand the split second. He claims that he understands and you [pointing to previous visitor] claim that you don't understand. [Laughter] And I can say both are understanding. Even when you think you don't understand, you have to understand. So there's understanding. There is no problem. And he understood, so there is understanding here and understanding there. In nature there is no difference. That's all!

Q [Another visitor]: I see that theoretically...

K: Judy just wants to survive!

Q [Another visitor]: I thought Ramana wrote that it has to be somebody or something to see this non-happening...

K: Judy still thinks that when she is realized there will be one who is realized. That's your problem. She thinks here [pointing to himself] is someone who understood something and there [pointing to the visitor] is someone who didn't understand. That's all and that's the survival system of little Judy because that makes Judy different to something else. By that difference, it survives as a different being.

Q [Another visitor]: Isn't it that for a relative body, the shift needs to happen to express itself...

K: The shift will happen anyway.

Q: But if there's no relative being, there is no talking about it. If Karl's body was not here, there wouldn't be any talking...

K: Of course there would be talking...

Q: Other talking but not this...

K: There are so many loud speakers on earth who talk permanently, they don't need Karl to talk. Consciousness doesn't need this body to talk – come on!

Q: At any moment, every particle in this universe is needed for the Self to be whatever. If we take this particle [pointing to Karl] out, there will be something missing...

K: There is not even one particle...

Q: There are infinite particles...

K: There are not even infinite particles. Now you make it really stupid.

Q: [Another visitor]: When you say that there is no Ramana or no Buddha who realized...

K: They all said that...

Q: In the relative level...

K: There is no relative level.

Q: There are seven ways of realization and three are relative levels...

K: Three experiences of separation but by that experience of separation, there is no separation – as there was never any relative level.

Q: When you say consciousness is looking for itself, it's all the time impersonal...

K: It is never impersonal. It doesn't even know impersonal and personal. Why should it be impersonal? You cannot give any attribute to That. By making it impersonal, you already create it as an opposite to personal.

Q: In the way you are experiencing yourself...

K: I don't experience myself – Thank God! I can never experience what I Am, so I can never experience myself. Hallelujah! That's all I can say.

Q: If consciousness will always look for itself, doesn't it mean that there is someone at a personal level, who experiences that I Am not the game?

K: That what I Am never experienced anything.

Q: In this way of realizing oneself, if something is experienced at the relative level, it could be that the person is experiencing the non-happening...

K: How can something that is an experience, experience something? Come on, get serious.

Q [Another visitor]: For me, the most challenging thing with you is not that you contradict yourself, but behind that there is a solid block of concrete that you cannot do a fucking scratch on it. That's the real annoying thing for me...

K: Everyone wants to scratch that. I always point to that which can never be touched.

Q: But what is it?

K: I have no idea. I talk to you and I see the same. That what is what-you-are is as solid as it can be. For me it makes no difference, but you are in the impression that you can be touched or changed like a leaf in the wind and of course you feel controlled by something. But in what I Am there is no believer, no belief system that can be moved by something.

But if I look at you, I see the same – the unmovable. It's always there. There's always that and nothing else as the unmovable itself. So I cannot even take it as a compliment because for me there is only That, but why not? Give me compliments. You cannot help me with that either.

Q [Another visitor]: That what you call unmovable, is what others would call God?

K: Call it underwear – forget it.

Q: But what is meant by That?

K: Call it That which has no second and the absence of the second which cannot be touched by anything. Not even by itself. So, call it whatever.

Q: What is this 'disappearing in the light'? Is it the light of Awareness or something else?

K: There is only light of awareness, what else can be there? The so-called fire swallows the spark that can be named and then the fire just assimilates that. The bigger takes over the little. So many books talk about the fire, grace eating up the little spark. Even the fire of spark which was not different from the fire itself – just gets lost. Maybe that's the bloody split second she wants to know. [Laughter]

Q: Have all the so-called realized persons seen this light?

K: No person ever saw this light. The moment the light is seen, there is no seer left. Whoever claims that he saw the light, for sure didn't see the light.

Q: It's a relative light?

K: Yeah. Like a bulb...

Q: What is this recognizer? In this [pointing the thumb], this [pointing his index finger] and this [pointing his middle finger]. The understanding is here [pointing the thumb], here [pointing the index finger] and here [pointing the middle finger]...

K: Understanding is uninterrupted.

Q: Yes, but what is this understanding?

K: Different.

Q: It's information...

K: No. It's different understanding.

Q: Different from what?

K: Different understanding. Understanding of form, understanding of non-form and even the understanding of awareness or origin of form and formless. All that is understanding in different ways.

Q: Different ways of what?

K: There is no what. Different ways of realization. It's all shifting between different understandings. You can even call it knowledge of the body, the knowledge of spirit and knowledge of awareness, of light.

Q: And this [closes his fist] also?

K: That is knowledge without experiencing itself.

Q: But knowledge without one is not possible to understand...

K: There is understanding but no one who understands anything. It is not understanding in action. That is total non-action of understanding. This [opening his thumb, index and middle fingers] is understanding in action. [closing his fist] This is non-beingness, but even in non-beingness, energy is That what is non-beingness. That's all.

Q: For me this experience [closes his fist] is the first experience...

K: For who? For you? I said these [opening his thumb, index and middle fingers] are three different ways of experiencing yourself as being That.

Q: But this [closes his fist] is not experience?

K: This is what-you-are without an experience. It is simply pointing to That what never needs to experience itself to be itself. You don't need to experience anything to be what-you-are, that's the pointer.

Q: But understanding this experience...

K: Understanding doesn't need to understand anything to be understanding and understanding in action is understanding of that [opening his thumb], that [opening his index finger] and that [opening his middle finger].

Q: But this [closes his fist] is also a conclusion...

K: It's not a conclusion. It's just that every night in absolute absence of any experience you exist. That's all.

Q: But this [closes his fist] is also information...

K: There is no information in That. This [opening his thumb] is the first information which is no-information – [opening his thumb] the information of light, [opening his index finger] the information of space-like spirit and [opening his middle finger] the information of the world. All that is information but what is the origin of all that information?

Q: This is a conclusion. Is it not possible to experience That [opening his thumb]...

K: Of course it is possible to experience That. Every morning you experience That – to be prior to the notion of 'I', you-are – already. Already here you switch between the three. There is no conclusion in it. Without Awareness, without I Amness, without body experience, there will be no awareness, no I Amness and no body experience. This is the knowledge of heart [closes his fist]. Come on, this is not conclusion, it's an absolute concrete fact. You want to get it here. That's your conclusion.

Q: For me it's impossible to know something without experience...

K: For 'you'! As you say for Constantine – he needs experience, but That what is Absolute existence, never needs to experience anything to be what-it-is. You're right. For the phantom you think you are, it needs to experience something, but not for That what is Reality. Come on!

As you said – for 'me'! But who is this bloody 'me' who needs something that depends on experiences? That's Contantine. You just confirmed what I said. Every ghost needs an experience of other ghost-like experiences to exist and it cannot imagine that it can exist without any ghost-like experience.

But that there can be a ghost at all, prior to that, the ghost has to be That, what is without the ghost and you cannot deny that. Even by denying That, you point to that there has to be someone, that is prior to that who is denying something. You just confirm that you exist permanently, which never needs any confirmation anyway. But you still permanently confirm yourself.

You want to go with your rational intellect into it and that is impossible. By that you can only say that 'I can only come to the conclusion that without me there is no experience'. And that what is 'me' always needs an experience. So even the experience of the absence of experience – is a phantom.

Who is the experiencer of what is in the absence of an experience, experiencing That what is the absence of the experience? Can you follow? I see you cannot, no one can follow That – not even me. You just go from there to there to there and nothing happens. That's actually the split second, you always shift between all the three and for what-you-are nothing happened by shifting.

So be happy that nothing happens by all those shifts. You cannot gain or lose anything even by being in that bloody light of awareness. Your nature does not gain anything. It always shifts back to the experience of this world and experiencing the spirit. What is the problem?

Q: No problem!

K: Just enjoy it because this will always happen – shifting between all the shifts and nothing ever happens. Even if I say there are seven different possibilities, you will always shift between them infinitely and nothing will ever happen.

So you can be here in the relative experience, as you can be in the Absolute tra...la...la... or not, for what-you-are in nature it makes no difference and I can only point to That. The quality of your existence does not depend on the way you experience anything. You have nothing to gain to go into the seventh or lose by staying in the first. You don't lose anything here and you don't gain anything there. Because you are not a loser and you are not a gainer. You are That what is life – which has nothing to lose in any way of experiencing itself. Come on!

You see the light in the end of the tunnel and you run for it, that keeps you busy. The light 'carrot'.

Q: The light 'carrot' is very tasty...

K: But it's never as tasty as That what never needs to taste itself to be itself. The tastelessness of what-you-are. Nothing is as tasty as That. Even the light experience is bitter compared to That tastelessness of your existence.

Q: For now, that's enough for me...

K: Eat it until you vomit! [Laughter] Even *prana* cannot satisfy you – but you can try.

Q: Drink the nectar from the feet of Vishnu...

K: And then you become a slave of the nectar of Vishnu.

Q: Not this [pointing his thumb] but this [closing his fist]...

K: Vishnu is already this [pointing his thumb] one.

Q [Another visitor]: This what is called split-second, is it same as recognition?

K: No, it's not a recognition. It's the Absolute knowledge that what you can-be, cannot be known – which was always there and is not something new. Splitting the second is destroying the hope, that by whatever, you can know yourself. That's the split second.

Q: So the split-second is the recognition that the phantom never existed?

K: No. It's simply being what-you-are – that's the split second and by being what-you-are – everything-is. There is nothing but what-you-are and that is splitting the second and not by any other thing you can split the second. Just by being what-you-cannot-not-be and that is what-is. That is splitting the second – the idea of duality. Just by being what-you-are and not by anyone who is splitting the second.

Q: But at that moment also...

K: There is no moment! This cannot be in any moment. Because the moment already is the second and splitting the second is like there was never anything as what-you-are. You are that what-is and that what-is-not recognized by anyone. You just are That!

Q: Even when recognition happens, there is someone who recognizes...

K: Absolutely! And that can only be relative.

Q: And recognition can only be of light or...

K: In the first three [states of consciousness], there is recognition.

Q: And after that, it's split-second?

K: This [closing his fist] is the end of the recognizer. This is the end of the beginning.

Q: And the split-second is the end of the recognizer?

K: It's the end of the beginning. Because without a beginning, there is no recognizer. So, the end is the end of the beginning and in that Absolute end, there was never any beginning. So nothing ever happened for what-you-are. There was never any – just pointers!

Q: Just pointers of after?

K: That's the problem, there is no 'after', because for That, there was no before and for That there is no after. That is splitting the second because when there is no time at all, never was, never will be. Because time is the idea of the mind, which is the idea of separation. There is 'one' who recognizes something else or even himself. Even recognizing himself is two.

So, the end of recognition is what-you-are and the end of recognition is the end of recognizer, recognizing something which can only be relative and the end of the recognizer, recognizing something is the beginning of what-you-are, but where you begin, everything else ends. This cannot be mixed and you cannot get closer to That. This is like the dream ends where you start and where you end the dream starts. You never went into the dream, so you cannot get out of the dream whatever is in the dream cannot enter what-you-are. There is a total – No!

Q: Sometimes it sounds like it is happening in time from the mind position…

K: From your position, something happens. Because the Absolute happening is the end of your happening.

Q: I think what everyone wanted to ask was – How does this happening change the perception of the body-mind organism?

K: [Laughing] Perception is not changed by That – that is important. You can make a road that this is the end of fear, this is the end of idea that you can die, this is the end of the beginning. As I said, when there is no beginning, there is no end. But there is no 'one' who recognizes That. There is no realized 'one' created by That. There is no someone who claims that I know more than you. That is why I never claim that I know more than anyone else here. In a relative way, for sure, I know something else – but not more.

Q [Another visitor]: Something else, means something!

K: Of course! The end of the end. What makes you look for something or expect something? It's your hope for a happy end. Everyone is hoping for enlightenment as a happy end, where the 'I' ends and there is only happiness.

Q: No one could come up with an idea that people who proclaimed to be enlightened, couldn't tell that…

K: But even they speak from enlightenment position. It needs two and it's still confirming separation. [Mocking] If I would tell you from this position that I'm in the God consciousness and you are in the pig stall of existence, you have to join that where I Am and you have to listen to me so that you can join that. Then you can say that I'm in a better position than you.

Q: But you always say you are in a better position than me…

K: I never say that I'm in any position.

Q: But no one believes you...

K: Doesn't matter, I still say it. What can I do? As I say That what-you-are never needs any advantage to be what-it-is. What else can I do? I'm seeing the absolute advantage of life, which never needs any advantage in life. You talk from a relative life which needs an advantage. What else can I do except present you That what-you-are never needs any advantage and I can just repeat it, just point to it. Whatever advantage you can reach will never be enough, I can only point to That.

Q: But cannot this [pointing to Karl] talk from any relative position?

K: No! I cannot talk from any position. You listen from a relative position. When you are in the dream, you talk out of the dream into the dream.

Q: But am I always in the dream?

K: No. You imagine to be in the dream and by your almighty nature, you imagine to be in the dream, you imagine to be born, your reality imagines as being born. An imaginary being which is born, that's your reality right now and that makes you the Almighty. And whatever the Almighty imagines and then imagines to be an entity that is born, it becomes the reality. That is the nature of being the Almighty. Imagine! And then the split-second is That what is imagining everything but it can never be imagined.

Q: Split-second is cutting off the imagination?

K: It is cutting off the imagination, that you are something that can be imagined.

Q: How to cut it off?

K: There is no one who can do that. Just by you being That what-you-are, everything is imagined, but is never part of it. No one can do that, but every one is it – already. That's the problem.

But by you trying to imagine That, you even make That, as an imaginary object. And if I tell you be happy that you cannot find yourself in any imagination, this is a pointer that you are not an 'image' or even 'not an image'.

Because you-are, all that is, but you are not because of That.

Q: What is this imagination?

K: Ramana says that you are the Absolute dreamer. The Absolute dreamer starts dreaming and next what he is dreaming is – being the world. But prior to the dreamt dreamer, already the Absolute dreamer is and that is your nature. As an Absolute dreamer, you never went dreaming for that what-you-are.

So nothing happened to That, what is the Absolute dreamer. So in the presence and the absence of the dreamt dreamer – you are what you are. So you always start as a dreamer, as a creator, then you create what can be created. But prior to creator, is that what is – with and without the creator and that is not an image.

And already by imagining the creator, there the separation starts. The creator is different from what is created. But what-you-are is already there, before even the imagination of the creator happens or the experience of the creator happens – You are That! And That never went out of what-it-is, never lost its nature. By none of this imaginary dream-like actions you can attain That.

Q: When you say that, I sort of understand and agree...

K: And then eat another understanding, another understanding like a little wood-pecker going through some hard wood – understanding, understanding, understanding. Until maybe in hundred thousand years, it breaks through. You have all the time in the world. I said 'may be'

Q [Another visitor]: But maybe it's more quicker, maybe 99999...

K: But you will break through. Do you know the story of the two seekers sitting under a tree and then came an enlightened one and they ask him – You must know when will we get enlightened and he says – Yes, you will be enlightened in a as many life times that there are leaves on this tree. One starts crying – 'Poor me', like some over here and the other one gets exited – Yes! I will get enlightened and all the leaves from the tree fall.

I can just give the message – that the imaginary veil of imaginary existence came to you and it will be gone. Who cares how long it takes? The ignorance came and the ignorance will be gone one day and this is the split-second – that you see that it arrived and it will depart. So what? And you are still what-you-are.

Q [Another visitor]; That sounds easy...

K: It is easier than you imagine, but you trying to do it, is impossible. To be it – is easy, to become it – is impossible. The tendency is trying to become it, but by trying to become it, you will wait forever, because you will never become it. No one will ever be it, but everyone is it.

The wishlessness can never be reached by any wish. But you are now wishing the wishlessness to happen and the very wish is your imaginary idea that you can reach something. The wish came and the wish will be gone one day and you still will be what-you-are, like this body came to you and one day it will be gone. Then the next comes and then it will be gone again.

So, things come, things go, images arrive, images depart. The image of the world comes and goes, the image of the spirit comes and goes and even light comes and goes. So even the light of *Shiva* is fleeting. But for there to be something fleetin – you have to be what-you-are.

Q [Another visitor]: So from what you said before, from one life to another, something is improved?

K: No. I didn't say that. It's not an improvement. In one of the instances, the Self drops everything – even the idea of Self. But that is inspite of how many life times you have had, there is no improvement in it.

Q: It's always inspite...

K: That's what I say from the beginning, it's inspite.

Q: Now I like 'inspite' but before I didn't like this idea at all. It took three months of listening to 'inspite' every day...

K: Your bloody mother, keeps you away from being what-you-are – by being a son of a barren woman. That's why they make it thousands of life times. In one case the reaction is 'Oh I never will!' and in another case 'Oh I will!'. Unpredictable.

Q: Does this depend upon *vasanas*?

K: No. It doesn't depend on anything, whether the Self is enjoying it or hating it. As I said yesterday, it absolutely enjoys it in heaven and absolutely hates it in hell. Both possibilities are always there and it cannot decide and it doesn't depend on *vasanas* or how the circumstance is.

Q: My *vasanas* are better than others...

K: Consciousness always compares with consciousness, of which one is bigger. It's an Olympic game of consciousness. Who jumps higher or lower? Who went higher into the experience of understanding and who went deeper into the realization of his nature? And then they sit somewhere and compete. Fantastic!

Q [Another visitor]: I love the fact that everyone's nature is the same...

K: Call it stupid, but everyone is stupid.

Q [Another visitor, laughing]: She really likes that everyone is as stupid as I am...

K: That's fun! We are one in stupidity. As no one can know himself, he must be very stupid and I sit here and tell you, enjoy the stupidity – that's all. Because it will never change. You are knowledge, which will never know itself and from the relative position, it must be stupid. It cannot know itself – How stupid can it be? But from that position of knowledge, it is absolute. Because even knowledge doesn't know there is knowledge, or who has to know itself or not. So the absence of anyone who is or is-not, is not so bad. Not good either, but not so bad.

Q: Ramesh would always say, we're playing our role perfectly...

K: Perfection plays perfect roles, but the best role it plays is playing stupid. [Laughter] It even claims to suffer about it! Always the Oscar – again and again. For this role – Consciousness perfectly played the role of stupid and today it plays the role – 'I know'. [Laughter]

Q [Another visitor]: So it can play role of being intelligent. But is it intelligence?

K: Yeah. When there is intelligence, there is intelligence. When there is no-intelligence, there is no-intelligence. This is the joy of being absolute irrelevant. Happy or unhappy, grumpy or not grumpy. Thoughtful! [Laughter]

Q [Another visitor]: When the talk went on, in the beginning I could see the identification with the phantom and at certain times, there was a shift happening. There was an understanding but it was not something that I could repeat. There was a clear notion of understanding something, but not in the normal way of understanding...

K: And it never goes into the memory. There is a presence without a memory, it cannot be repeated.

Q: Yeah. And at the same moment when it switches back to this one [body], there is no possibility to understand or put it to words or anything. It is just absolutely impossible, at least to the perception that is here [pointing to himself]...

K: Yeah, we can talk about it but it cannot be talked. This absolute unpronounced 'yes' is permanently there. Even now when you shift again to the relative, it's still there. It's never-never.

Q: It became quite clear by seeing the 'shift' that constantly seems to happen...

K: It happens. Then it goes here and it goes back.

Q: But most of the time the attention here [pointing to body] is on the phantom entity...

K: Again and again. As helplessness cannot stay, it shifts back, but what's the difference? You just have to know yourself as That and then shifting here doesn't change anything. So you perceive That unmovable and the movable, but both is perceived. By what? There is no one! There is just a perception of the unmovable, unpronounced and then the experience of the movable, pronounceable. Both are experiences, but there is no experiencer you can find. So neither in the unpronounced, or the pronounced you can find yourself because you can shift always. That what is shifting is not changed by that 'shift'.

Q: But what was aware of that 'shift'?

K: That, what is awareness. Is there anyone who is aware? No. You cannot find anyone who is aware, but there is awareness. There is awareness of the shift between the relative and the non-relative and there is awareness about that shift, but there is no one who moved in that. There is no movement from there to there, it just shifted by itself but not by any intention. There is no basic intention by anyone. It's just automatic shift in different ways of experiencing yourself.

This way of relative experiencing is there and then there is a shift automatically that goes to that unpronounced, which knows by itself. Then again here and then go further – maybe, but that what is shifting, is never shifted by that. That's the way you dream changes. There is a dream of non-understanding, then there is a dream of understanding which is unmovable. But even that is a dream. Because even that you can say – this is different to That and whatever is different is not it. Because That is better, there is quite a stillness there. The stillness of understanding, which is better than the so-called movable understanding of ignorance – but even That is not it.

So the seer is not different by seeing this relative or that non-relative. Your nature cannot be changed by it. You don't have to stay there, to be what-you-are. That's more like a pointer to the split-second, that you are in the awareness that you are in the ignorance of the daily life of what-you-are. By none of these differences, you are different in nature. Your nature cannot be made different by any of those experiences.

So you can shift infinitely between all of that and by all the shifts of differences of experiences, you can never be changed, or gain or lose anything. Because what-you-are, is not more there or less here. That's the quality of life which has nothing to gain or to lose by any experience. So what's more natural as being That, which by being all of that, is unchangeable. Never gaining or losing anything.

So you didn't lose anything by the experience of being born, or with the feeling of being born, or with the feeling of being the un-born. So even the experience of being the unborn is unreal. Reality is never-never. If you would be the unborn, the experience of the unborn, would be more real than the experience of being born. So there will still be one who makes a difference between that. By that difference, you suffer in a way – then this is always better than that.

No, this is not better than that, both is ignorance and only that what-you-are is knowledge – which is shifting infinitely, but by all that shifting or understanding or non-understanding or whatever you can experience, it can never be changed more or less to what-it-is. And that is knowledge itself – which is never more or less than it is. So be happy!

Q: Does the shift happen with intention?

K: There is a helplessness of your nature. You cannot have the intention before the intention happens. The shift happens by itself. You cannot prevent yourself from shifting.

Q: When shifting to this relative, it's always...

K: By being what-you-are, what-you-are has nothing to gain here, the shift happens or not. There is a carelessness of shifts, it may or may not happen – who cares? That's the meaning of who cares? If the shift happens from here, to the understanding or to the ignorance. Who cares about it? You only care because you think it's better there than here.

Q: But the caring happens only when it shifts back...

K: There is a caring happening, but by that caring there is no care-taker. The caring happens by itself, the worrying happens by itself. But where is the worrier? Who worries? There is worrying only because you imagine that not caring is better than caring. That makes you an imaginary care-taker who is imagines that by that what is understanding, you are closer to what-you-are than by non-understanding. That makes you one who depends on understanding.

But your nature is knowledge that never needs any understanding to be what-it-is or non-understanding. You are in the understanding and in the non-understanding – That and that what can gain something – there is a gainer and a loser in the same moment. But what-you-are can never gain or lose anything by any so-called imaginary dream-like experiences. So be happy!

And I can only repeat it – again and again and again. I can only point that there is nothing to gain from whatever you experience – or to lose.

Q [Another visitor]: If this is not better, being this [pointing to the body] than being that...

K: I never said that. I said the experience of this is not better than the experience of that. I didn't say you are this or that. By the experience of this or the experience of that – what-you-are cannot lose or gain anything, but no one is this and no one is that.

Q: So the experience of this is not better than the experience of that...

K: Yeah. It's both the experience of quality.

Q: But you are always hitting so hard on that...

K: Yeah, so that you may go to that experience and realize that it's not a better experience there. Because now you still believe, That is better than this. I destroy this, so that you may experience That and then in the split-second, you may experience what-you-are here is what-you-are there and it makes no difference.

Q [Another visitor]: So the split-second is eternal absolute...

K: There was never any second to split my dear. So there cannot be an eternal split-second. It sounds nice but how can you split something which is not even there?

Q: In last fifteen minutes, we talked that may be that is the split-second...

K: Yeah, we talked about the 'may be' and 'may be' is always a 'may be' – So what? You want to be a 'may be' or you want to be That what-you-are? It's always dangerous if someone claims to have understood something. Always trying to kill the second which is not there.

Q: Tricky...

K: Yeah, it's very tricky. It's a permanent trap – that you try to get rid of something which is not even there. The moment you wake up, you are the trapper, the trapping and the trapped and you are always being trapped by being the trapper, the trapping and the trapped. The eternal trapper, eternal trapping and the eternal trapped.

And who cares to be trapped by what one is? Being trapped in that what is freedom itself – the absence of the second, who cares about being trapped in the trap of oneself? Or being addicted to oneself – who cares about it? Say it...

Q: ME!

K: Yeah, you see [laughter] – all the me's. And the 'me' is the wish to know oneself and it will never end.

Q: Some years ago, you said that is better than this...

K: I still say it's better, but it's not good enough – I always say that too. That's a paradox you cannot break.

Q: Yesterday I went in time and the food was nice, for sure better than this food...

K: And if you come from four weeks of eating shit, this food would be heaven. [Laughter] The differences will never end, as you never end.

Q: It's the same in life...

K: There's no life in this life. In this imaginary life, are imaginary differences, by an imaginary phantom who makes differences. There are tendencies of tongue, that which can taste some differences, is already a sickness. Then by taking that as real, the sickness continues. Having a body is already a disease. Who said it? Your master Ramana. Who cares when this disease ends?

Q [Another visitor]: This information is already here. [pointing to his body] So if I have a question, I'm either adding more to it without confirming my dad [genes]. But even knowing that, either way it's a split-second...

K: It's a relative knowing and it will not help you and the questioner will always have questions and not having questions, is still questionable. So there will always be questions again. But your nature, your origin, never has any questions.

Q: So, either way it doesn't affect what-is...

K: No. The origin never has any questions, never needs any answers. But that what is an imaginary questioner, will always have questions. Then an imaginary seeker, not seeking, is still a seeker and an imaginary questioner not questioning anything, is still a questionable questioner – not questioning anything.

Q: So, I can pretend that I have questions...

K: You have them anyway. The doubtless doubter is still doubtful. The non-seeking seeker is as much a seeker as before. That what can end, can start again. But for what-you-are which never had any questions about what-it-is and what-it-is-not, never needs any answer. But that what-is – is already an imaginary phantom...

Q: So, no waiting for a happy ending then...

K: There was never any happy beginning and there will never be any happy ending. But this is the absolute end of what you imagine to be – may be. Again, we are back to the split-second. Because only by that imagination that one day you have no questions anymore, because you would know yourself, you continue that and you are in the relative expectation game. In so-called absolute shift, which is not a shift, splitting the second is just being That what never had any question and never will have any answer to what-it-is. Never needed one, anyway. So the absolute needlessness of existence never demands anything – to-be or not-to-be.

Q: So the 'other' is so-called staying alive...

K: The 'other' is a permanent survival system running – always defining himself. So the imaginary definer who wakes up, already tries to define himself. Defines himself as a body, as a spirit, as awareness and then shifting between That. That's the definer. But none of that is fine enough for him and there is no fulfillment in one of them and only to be That what never needs fulfillment – is fulfillment. To be That – what never needs to be fulfilled to be what-it-is. This paradox you cannot solve.

Absolute satisfaction is being That what is *sat*, but That what is *sat* doesn't know any *sat*. That is satisfaction itself and doesn't know any satisfaction – never needs to be satisfied. Never needs to fight for itself.

Q: *Sat* without *chit* and *ananda*...

K: There is only *sat* – there is no shit *ananda*. Otherwise if you put it together it becomes *sat-shit-ananda*. Such a shit is *ananda*. Then you make a circumstance where you only can be what-you-are, a circumstance of *sat-chit-ananda* – the Self being aware of the Self. In the self-awareness you can only be the Self which is in the self-awareness – only then can you be in the *ananda* of being self-aware! But then you again make yourself dependent on the bloody awareness.

There are three different names of what-you-are. One is *sat*, one is *chit* and another one is *ananda*. But none of them knows himself and none of them needs to know itself as what-they-are to be what-they-are. So, you are *sat*, you are *chit* and you are *ananda*, but you don't need *sat-chit-ananda*.

February 11, 2009
Coimbatore

SEE YOU AGAIN – NEXT TIME

Q: Is it possible to do something to not get identified with this story?

K: Try hard.

Q: But are you hammering us so that...

K: For sure not. You can stay identified forever and no one cares.

Q [Another visitor]: She cares...

K: Yeah, but she's the only one who cares. No one else cares that she cares.

Q: I heard some people saying that by being with you quite a while, life becomes easier...

K: Especially in your case. When we met her years ago, she was so down, she had just buried her last husband and now look at her!

Q: It's because that time has passed, it's not because of you... [Laughter]

K: You are really like an advertisement for me. A negative advertisement, after all those years nothing happens! You prove what I say – that it's absolutely irrelevant, whatever I do.

Q: It looks like...

K: As I always say, you are not here for an advantage. But you are here for an advantage, that's not my problem, that's only your problem.

Q: I'm here because I can't help it. I'm helpless...

K: But I didn't talk about that. You sit here for having an advantage and I cannot help you for that.

Q: I just wanted to make sure that there is nothing that I missed...

K: You missed everything. There were infinite possibilities but you missed all of them.

Q: And I will also miss it in future?

K: You will miss the next thousand years of opportunities – be happy! Thousands and thousands of lifetimes, you will miss yourself. Then more thousands and thousands of lifetimes, you will still miss yourself.

Q: The experience of this and the experience of That, this is not higher than That, but this is better. But you said again and again yesterday that this is better...

K: That's better for the relative phantom.

Q: That is a relative phantom...

K: No, no! Even this is a relative phantom. These are three different positions [opening his thumb, index and middle fingers] of the relative phantom.

Q: And the experience of oneness?

K: The experience of oneness is the second [opening his index finger]. This [raising his thumb] is already the experience of awareness, the choiceless awareness. There is not even oneness anymore. The body, the oneness and the awareness – these are the three phantom states and the best is awareness state – *samadhi*.

Q: Are there bridges from one state to another?

K: Yeah, there are bridges, but no one can walk them. There are many bridges, but no one can take them. Ferries, ferry-men, boats from one shore to the other shore.

Q: So the last one is not higher but it's better?

K: It is better for the phantom.

Q: But it's not good enough?

K: No. It will not make you what-you-are.

Q: What I Am is prior and beyond?

K: It is inspite of it.

Q: And there is also no bridge?

K: There is absolutely no bridge. From first to third there are bridges. Some teachers can help you – maybe.

Q: Just to phrase it – I can't do anything...

K: You can do whatever you like, but you cannot decide what you like.

Q: I cannot decide that I can go from the identified to the non-identified?

K: No. You always want to go to the highest. That you cannot avoid. This decision is already made. The tendency is always to the highest from that relative phantom. It's always a tendency of the highest. There's always a carrot – the enlightenment carrot – the highest. That's already decided, you don't even have to worry about it. This decision is already made. Now you try to do your best.

Q: That feeling makes me so crazy sometimes if I could just know the right thing, I would do it and I don't believe or trust if you say you can't do anything...

K: I didn't say that. I said you can do whatever you like but you cannot like what you like or not like. It will happen anyway – whatever you jump to. Enjoy the ride, it's already arranged. The ticket is paid, no direction home. So enjoy the ride.

Even Maharishi Mahesh Yogi said to George Harrison. If you don't know where you want to go to, all the ways get you there where you don't want to be.

Q [Another visitor]: All things must pass...

K: It has already passed when you experience it.

Q: Is the *shruti* still one when the mind is jumping?

K: Ramana talks about the flat line of the *shruti*, like the awareness line.

Q: And that's the base of everything?

K: When you wake up in the morning, that's the first and just to stay there in that awareness is the technique they all used. *Shruti* is the basic tone, the basic sound of *Om*, staying there and from there all the orchestral, universal information system of sounds are always there. But you just are That – by staying there. That's what they mean by canvas where all the projections, information, differences are projected and it doesn't make you more or less as That.

So that's the first and the last you can experience. Then you just don't move from there. You abide in the first and the last notion. Even that is maybe an effort in the beginning, but after a while, it becomes your nature.

Q [Another visitor]: Makes sense...

K: Ramana talked a lot about it. That you just stay in that awareness and after a while it becomes so natural that you don't have to make any effort to stay there. But in the beginning he says that it needs an effort of putting awareness, being awareness, meditation of awareness. Right now, your home is your body. Then maybe after meditation, your home becomes your spirit – the space.

Then even after more effort, you end up in that first and last. Then there is still a little effort to stay there. But after a while, maybe that becomes your nature and if awareness is your nature, there is timelessness. No phantom can stay there and then there is no problem anyway. Just by the nature of presence-absence of what-you-are, even that becomes...

Q [Another visitor]: It's a placard that one can relax in the nature of as it is...

K: No, it's a trick. What-you-are doesn't need it but to get rid of the phantom idea...

Q: Just seeing that somehow, realizing that...

K: But you always fall in the trap of falling in love again. So how to kill that falling in love? This tendency of love. Because that tendency always brings you out again into that movement. You follow your tendency of love and you want to...whatever.

Q: So maybe it just wears out eventually, there is no way of doing that...

K: Yeah. If you see it like that, then you are already aware that it came and it will go. That's what is meant by 'all things must pass' – the tendencies come and go. In that awareness, you are already aware That what-you-are is not part of the coming, fleeting, experience. Staying in that awareness is already being awareness. Because that what is awareness, never comes, never goes. By that you wouldn't attain what-you-are, but maybe the phantom disappears.

Q: Irrelevant...

K: Yeah. Like ceasing away. Because there is no second and without a second, there is no holding on to anything. No time, no mind, no intellect and there is simply no place for any phantom. But sounds good! So we can make some techniques. How to go there? How to stay there?

And imagine, all that happens by itself! Even the effort is already decided. It will never be your effort. That's what I try to tell her, the effort you will make is already there. If it's not there, it will not happen and what has to happen, will happen anyway. But that what is not going to happen, will never happen. So, you can just relax in that, but she still believes that she can decide how the future will be.

Q: That tendency is there anyway...

K: Yeah. All that understanding, all what happens is already decided. That's Ramana's famous saying – 'Whatever has to happen, will happen. Whatever is not meant to happen, will not happen'. As much as you try or not, even trying is already in-built. It doesn't depend on anyone. It's an absolute freedom of – That. Freedom from one who can or needs any energy to change anything.

So not even God can change that. So every word I say is already... Even the claiming of that word, someone is there who claims to have said that is already there. If it just has to happen, it will happen. If there is no one left to claim it, even that is already there.

Every moment is an absolute agreement. The whole totality agrees to what you do. Without that total agreement, you could not even lift your eyebrow. Without that acceptance of totality, there is no possibility of any smallest action. That is called helplessness of... whatever. Totality has no advantage of what happens.

Q [Another visitor]: I believe this totally, but at the same time, in the beginning the idea was that it is my effort. But everyday this idea was changing and it was more clear that it was not by me. So something comes...

K: But it needs one who realizes the change. In the beginning, you are the absolute doer, you do it. Then more and more doer-ship is chiseled away until you become the non-doer and things just happen by themselves.

Q: In the beginning I had this idea that it's my effort and now it's that it comes by itself and not by my effort...

K: But now it's 'not your effort'.

Q: No...

K: But there is still 'one' who makes no effort. So, you own now the non-effort. That belongs to you.

Q: But earlier, it was my effort...

K: It's just a shift between one who is doing something and then you are in the non-doing doer. And then?

Q: I don't know...

K: So what then? When you enter the non-doership.

Q: There is a change. In one way it's incredible, it comes when it comes...

K: [Laughing] You're blissed when it comes and you're pissed when it doesn't come.

Q: Yeah...

K: In the beginning you think it's your doing and now you accept whatever comes, but you still expect something to come.

Q: If you want to describe it in negative way, then yes...

K: It has to be negative.

Q: Why?

K: Because 'you' are there. First it's your doing and then you put all your hope on grace.

Q [Another visitor]: You talked about the *shruti*, the flat line of awareness. That's what Ramana would call the Self?

K: No, he doesn't call it the Self. The flat line is the position of peace in the so-called trinity of That. He doesn't call it the Self.

Q: And what he calls the Self is what-we-are?

K: It's inspite of That.

Q: So when he talks about *shruti*...

K: The *shruti* is called the I-I.

Q: When he says I-I, is he not talking about the Absolute?

K: That's the absolute, the 'eye' of the 'eye' and the 'I' of the 'I' is the 'I Am' of the 'I Am' and is 'world' of the 'world'. It's always a flat line.

Q: Which is that awareness?

K: No, it's not the awareness. It is that what is awareness and that what is I Amness and that what is the world. That is the flat line. It's not like staying in awareness. The absolute flat line, the unmovable solid block of existence is that what is the awareness, I Amness and the world. No one has to stay there. That's why it's called the effortlessness of being what-you-are.

But first it starts by you trying to become awareness of awareness, putting all awareness on awareness – by being awareness. And then you shift into that fourth state, into that absence of any presence and from there no one comes back. From the first three you always shift around. But putting total concentration on That what-you-are is putting awareness to awareness – by being awareness. By being awareness, there is a vertical now that no 'one' can exist in. No relative idea or concept can remain in that vertical now. By nature of awareness, by being awareness, it's like an ice block in the sun – melting away. Then it's just a question of time when there is no story left or even no-story.

So the ownership ceases away simply by being what-you-are as awareness – That what is awareness. UG [Krishnamurthi] would call it the calamity. That all the stories of the personal and the impersonal of all whatever happened or didn't happen, get burnt down in the calamity of the holocaust of the 'I'. It's a hell-fire for the devil, in which even the devil cannot survive. The idea of God cannot survive in That what is awareness. That becomes God, what doesn't know any God because the God doesn't know any God anymore.

So in the absolute not knowing of the God, by God being God. From That, no God arises. Then what is God is the 'I' of the 'I', the 'I Am' of the 'I Am' and the 'world' of the 'world'. The Absolute father, the Absolute spirit and the Absolute man. The Absolute – as That.

So the first three are like you shift around for one who has an advantage place. But by being the awareness of the awareness, already there is no 'one' who has an advantage in it. So what to do? And this is the story of all the sages, Jesuses and Buddhas and Ramanas. It's all the same story. There are seven ways of realization you have to realize yourself in.

Everyone was expecting that I would say awareness is better than the rest. That the awareness is like a flat line one can be in or being the flat line and the rest is different. That is the impression you get. Everyone got that impression.

Q [Another visitor]: If you look at the phantom and you investigate in that, what comes out is the is-ness. It doesn't matter where it is, it's always this and this and this and it doesn't matter if it's final or a flat line...

K: That's what I said last year, what-you-are is there [raising his thumb], there [opening his index finger] and there [opening his middle finger] what-it-is, but there is no 'one' who is it. The phantom is the idea there is one who is awareness.

Q: But even there it doesn't matter...

K: We are not talking about that it doesn't matter. We're talking about that here is some kind of suffering running – of having an idea of what one is. That's the phantom idea – it's quite a sickness. There is a disease in it. That it doesn't matter is not the question for what-is, but for whatever is here, it matters, otherwise it would not sit here.

So to say it doesn't matter is a nice saying, but everyone wants to get rid of the phantom, because this mind, phantom, is suffering – from the beginning till the end. So we talk about how to get rid of it. So whatever you do to get rid of it, confirms that there is one who is in it. It doesn't work.

So you better be what-you-cannot-not-be and that is the only way of getting rid of whatever concepts and ideas you have about yourself. But not by any doer, meditation tra..la..la you can get rid of that what is the phantom. Because whatever you do, confirms that there is one who has to do something.

That is the trick of Ramana – put total concentration on That. Get into the concentration camp of – That, if you want to get rid of this and even that concentration cannot be done. So when Ramana said – it will happen that you feel depressed as if your head is pushed ten meters under water and there is no other way but to concentrate on what-you-are to get rid of the misery, it will happen if it's needed. If not, it will happen differently, but there is no one who can decide it. It will always be unique.

So, I don't deny the suffering here and the sufferer is quite real, when you believe in your so-called existence and everyone believes in it. Even this understanding doesn't matter because it's a fake one.

Q: I can only say whenever there is an investigation, the only thing what comes out is is-ness... 'it is' and 'it is' and 'it is'...

K: But is-ness is only in the dream. The is-ness is already a phantom. That's the Eckhart Tolle is-ness.

Q [Another visitor]: Could you expand on why the phantom is the is-ness?

K: Because it's an experience. As she said she always comes back to is-ness and the is-ness is already an experience. That maybe is the highest – but not high enough.

Q [Another visitor]: That's as far as I can go in the investigation...

K: Yeah, that is the end of investigation.

Q [Another visitor]: Then you know that this not it either...

K: No. It ends and what to do then? Many people end up in is-ness is all there is. Then they say truth is is-ness and is-ness is truth.

Q [Another visitor]: Then you make it a home...

K: Yeah and then you buy furniture for that home. Because you think now I found my final home. It's like Gangaji saying 'Welcome home!'. Welcome to the final healing of your soul. That's the is-ness she talks about.

Q [Another visitor]: And where does that fit in your...

K: Here [pointing his thumb]. Even if it's here, let it be here.

Q: So, you are saying being that is-ness...

K: When you are the is-ness, there is no is-ness anymore, but if you experience the is-ness, the is-ness is still mind. But this is the last that the intellect can present you. It's a final result of what comes of the investigation. This is the Eckhart's 'Now' – is-ness. I can only say again, it's not bad.

Q: But it is also like an experience to stay in that is-ness...

K: It's quite peaceful. That's why he calls it the Power Of Now. Just to see what it is not. One can talk about it, there is a vertical 'now' and it's quite a peaceful no-mind. I don't deny that.

Q [Another visitor]: When you call it peaceful do you mean that's *ananda*?

K: No. If that would be *ananda*, *ananda* would depend on the vertical experience. Whatever depends on any experience cannot be *ananda*.

Q: What you call – the suspension of mind...

K: Even that is not it. The no-mind is still not it.

Q: I remember one question that was asked to Ramana to make a distinction from finding the Heart and this suspension of the mind...

K: Finding the heart is being the heart. You always mix it up. The only stopping the mind is being the heart which doesn't know any heart. That's the full stop of existence. But there is no heart which knows heart anymore. So no one finds heart. He talks about that and not the way you talk about it.

Q: One person asked Ramana that in meditation his mind stops for half an hour and he had very peaceful moments...

K: It's a temporary peace.

Q: And Ramana said, it is nice but it's dangerous...

K: It's dangerous because you may end up thinking this is what-you-are. Then this may become very attractive. It's dangerous but it's another false experience.

Q: And Ramana said this not awareness. You need to stay all the time in awareness...

K: No. He says you have to put awareness permanently on awareness by being awareness and not staying in that. Again this is a wrong translation.

Q: For me this distinction is important because for some of us it felt like the suspension of the mind ...

K: It is the total suspension of the mind. But there is only one way of getting rid of the bloody mind, by being what-you-are and not by having a bloody no-mind experience.

Q: For me this difference is important, the temporary suspension of the mind and what you call 'You are the heart'...

K: There is no difference. What-you-are is even a difference in that difference and doesn't need to go and being the difference is what-you-are. But for what-you-are, there is no difference in the difference. That's the heart of the difference. So what's the problem?

Q [Another visitor]: What is the difference between staying in awareness and being awareness?

K: By being the awareness, there is no one who has awareness. There is no ownership of awareness. There is no 'your' awareness. When you are That what is the awareness, there is no 'my' awareness – that's a big difference, the absolute difference.

Q: And staying?

K: Staying is one too many.

Q: But who stays in awareness?

K: That is the question. Who can stay in awareness? And who needs to stay in awareness? So you better be awareness and then there is no 'one' who needs to stay.

Q: It is not possible to stay in awareness...

K: Some try and some claim that they can stay in awareness. They go to the *samadhi* and then 'they' are in *samadhi*.

Q: With the exclusion of the other two [body and the I Amness experience]?

K: They make the difference that it's a better place than the other experiences. It's like Shantimayi has to go to the Ganga and Ganga has to give her the energy so that she can go to that *samadhi* and get fresh air for her so-called nature. So she can get exhausted by her 'dear' disciples and her students. Then she needs to go to the Ganga and get enough energy from Ganga to recover from the painful surrounding of the students. Because maybe they don't pay enough donations, that she has to talk to the Ganga again. [Laughter] No one can talk to her at that time. 'Leave me all alone. If you see me, piss-off. I have to be with my mother Ganga. Now for some time, I can take you again and I'm only doing it for you'.

So she goes into that awareness or oneness, whatever you call it. It's like taking a bath and getting cleaned again because you're surrounded by so many dirty minds and dirty ideas, that you have to clean up again your 'inner nature', so that you can take it again. They call it purification in *vedanta*. The way of the *vedanta* is that you go to a place where you get purified. And staying in awareness is purification of your so-called 'light body'. Very nice! I have to always listen to people who come with all of that. I get taught, tortured.

Q [Another visitor]: We've just done a cleanse, so we can't be dirty...

K: Your mind is more dirty now than before because now you think you are purified. [Laughter] That's dirtiness itself when you think you're pure. They believe in it, you can't say they are lying. For them this is the reality – that awareness purification is needed when you're surrounded by so-called disciples and their dirty minds. Thank God I'm the dirty mind, I have no problem with it. No one can be more dirty than me.

Q [Another visitor]: The other day I read that when we are singing, we are in union with God...

K: Try hard! Go to a chorus in Germany, every second German is in a singing club in Germany. They drink and then they sing and then they are in union with God. [Laughter] That's why they call German *saufe's* [German for alcohol]. [Laughter] And Germans when they're drunk, they really start singing. When you drink enough, you drink yourself away and then you're in union of the coma with yourself.

Q: I didn't ask about drinking, I asked about singing...

K: But singing is the same, they're singing themselves away – in oneness. But in every bloody football stadium, there are people singing and screaming, a hundred thousand oneness – 'Goal'! There is no one left, there is no individual anymore, there is just – Goal! What's the problem with that? That's the same with singing. If you go to Shantimayi, there is nice singing and then you melt into that vibration of the sound.

Q: So, one sings to forget about oneself?

K: You forget the suffering. You only sing because you only want to avoid the separation. Because in singing you don't feel separated.

In that way, you don't suffer. It's temporary, it's like a drug. A temporary drug, which gets you out of separation, out of the disease of feeling not at ease.

Q [Another visitor]: It's like group meditation...

K: Dynamic meditation or whatever Osho did was all about it. Whatever you do, is getting rid of the doer. Even understanding, *jñana* yoga is all about that. Getting lost in working, getting lost in whatever, being workaholic is another drug. Whatever you do, is trying to get rid of the unbearable separation experience.

Q [Another visitor]: Osho said that meditation is the ultimate drug...

Q [Another visitor]: He said it's the ultimate medicine...

Q [Another visitor]: No. He said it's the ultimate drug. I have it in black and white...

K: What is the difference between medicine and drug? [Laughter] He said so many things; for sure he must have said it. Everyday he said something else. That's the only thing he did really right – contradicting himself moment by moment, next day he said totally different. So, what to do?

Q [Another visitor]: I didn't like that he used to give *shakti* and all of that...

K: It's a nice trick, like a magician. How to get the audience? You have to show some energy, you have to show some tricks, so that the audience comes. You show a flower, so that the beast may come and suck from you. That's the trick of all the pub owners and Osho was a pub owner who wants to attract more customers.

Q [Another visitor]: Some people had diarrhoea after that...

K: I hope! He was an *ayurveda* master. [Laughter]

Q [Another visitor]: Yesterday you talked about the black sun...

Q [Another visitor]: It's not easy to find the book on black sun...

K: It's rare because it's forbidden. It's about fascism and the Aryas from north of India.

Q [Another visitor]: And what do you say?

K: The black sun is the *swastika* – when it turns in the clockwise direction, it creates and when it turns the other way, it destroys. Then the black sun is the Self, what is in the absence of presence of an experience – that's the black sun, the darkness. When it turns in the right way, it is realizing itself, when it turns the other way, it becomes a black sun. So, the white sun and the black sun. It's like the yin and *yang* of the Tao. It's black in its nature, darkness, mystery. Then it turns the clockwise and it's realizing itself.

Q [Another visitor]: Once I had an experience, the *chakra* turning one way and then the *chakra* turning the other way…

K: It's the same, it's the solar plexus. It's like an 'S' or the opposite of 'S', it turns around and has an negative effect.

Q: I got the same impression, that one is building up and the other is destroying…

K: One is like a vacuum cleaner and the other one is going out – like a worm hole, creating or destroying just by the tendency. Like the spider that's spinning and the spider that's withdrawing. The withdrawing spider becomes the black sun. When it's spinning the net, it becomes the white sun.

Q [Another visitor]: Is it like a black hole?

K: It's just the perception creating and the perception withdrawing. It's not a black hole. Black hole would mean that particles would get sucked in. But this is not the case, no particles get sucked in there. It's like a creating energy and a destroying energy, but nothing gets created by creating and nothing gets destroyed by destroying. It's just perception imagining and perception getting into the darkness of non-perception.

Q [Another visitor]: Withdrawing…

K: From what? It's not a withdrawing.

Q [Another visitor]: So the Nazis knew about it?

K: The Aryas from north India knew about it.

Q: But did Adolf know about it?

K: They didn't know about it. The Thule society used that, not that they know about how it works. They abused it because only by religion you can make so many people go to war. So they abused that belief system, not that they knew that and Hitler was not a *jñani* or an *avatar*, but they played with it. It's an esoteric symbol. The Thule society was one of the biggest and it still is from the old Celtic and Indo-Germanic tradition.

Q [Another visitor]: Why is it forbidden to speak about it?

K: Because in Italy it is connected to the fascist movement. All the books are banned from the libraries. It's the same in Germany. Whatever you do with that, is like fascism. In that way you cannot see the *swastika* in Germany or Italy, but in America you find it more than in Germany or Italy.

Q [Another visitor]: They reversed it in Germany?

K: No. You find both in Tibet and India. It's just that you look at it from the other side, it is not reversed. It's just that you look at it from a different position. The reversed one is pointing to the black sun. When you look at it from that side, it represents darkness, mystery. From the other side, it is the light. So, one is the black *tantra* and the other one is the white *tantra*. The knowable, what you can know and what you cannot know and both is That.

But it depends upon where you look from. When you look at the solar plexus from the absolute side – it is black and if you look at it from the individual side – it is white. Because then you look at awareness. But when you look at that what is awareness, it's black.

Q [Another visitor]: When you spoke about the esoteric, it seems like they never went beyond...

K: They abused it, as Hitler abused it for his ideas. Because esoteric people want to make the world a better place and they need energy for that. Then they make a religion out of it. The whole Vatican is like black magicians – using some ideas of truth and God to control – with that religion. It's all the same.

Q [Another visitor]: At the moment of death is the movement of the *chakras* reversed?

K: Yeah. Perception withdraws...

Q: Could you see it in the movement of energy?

K: If you could see it, you could see a different direction. It's like an expression and a withdrawing. It's like energy gives life to this information of image and then it withdraws the energy. Then you see that it was already a corpse. When this energy, this perception goes out of it – nothing is left.

That I was fascinated with, when watching a pig. It was so obvious. Before there was a pig, very alive. Then his blood runs out, then the space becomes the energy of the pig and the energy is not gone, it simply went out of that information. So it's not a less energy there, not something less, no one got killed. It's just the energy of what is the energy, leaving what is information and everyone sitting here is just being alive by that energy. So that what is leaving the bodies are – That.

Q [Another visitor]: There was a physician in U.S. who had many workshops on this. He said he was working as a physician and he stopped by the bodies and he felt the energy...

K: The energy was creating and withdrawing...

Q: He didn't talk about the direction, but he said that you can feel the energy...

K: Yeah. The presence and then the absence.

Q: Even when the body is dead, the presence is still there...

K: The presence is still there, in emergency room, they see that. The presence just leaves the body and there is a space around it. The presence cannot go. It is just trapped into the body and then expands into the space or merging into that what is space anyway.

Q [Another visitor]: Energetically, is there a difference between somebody dying slowly by a disease?

K: When the virus is there, the perception goes more towards the space because you withdraw from that what is in this disease body. If you have extreme diseases, it withdraws more and more and then there is no pain anymore. You just go to a place where there is no pain anymore. If this (body) is painful, you just go to a space where there is no pain.

Q [Another visitor]: But I wonder to whom does this apply, only to humans or also the animals?

K: The elephants do the same. [Laughter]

Q: You also mentioned that when you were a kid, you had an experience when the pig was slaughtered suddenly there was a lot of space...

K: I just said that the energy from the pig went into the space and not that there was more energy.

Q: Does that apply to trees and stones?

K: Try to kill a stone. [Laughter] That's why you call a stone dead matter, but if you kill a mosquito, for sure there will be an amount of energy released. If you could see that, you would see the release of energy. Maybe you can cut your little finger and see a stream of light coming out.

Q: The energy is still there...

K: Yeah, when you cut your finger you still feel the whole arm because of the phantom experience. What is this phantom experience? It's just the energy which still forms the extension of the arm. Miracles! wonder! All of that, for sure, is the phenomenal side of energy.

That what is the energy of the sun is running everything – Whatever is here is running in different vibrations. The stone is in different vibration as you. The vibration of energy makes the stone very gross or someone more flexible, like a body or birds. It's all different vibrations but not of a different energy. The energy is not different. Just the expression is different.

Q: There are different expressions to the body. There is a meta body and there are different expressions of energy. Sometimes it sticks together and when somebody dies, the energy goes somewhere...

K: Not somewhere, it was already that what is energy that surrounded it. It's just concentrated energy. It's like if you pull the spark plug, the engine doesn't run anymore. Then you wouldn't call the engine dead since it does not run anymore. You put it together again and say now it's alive again.

It's the same with the body. If the fuse and everything is running, you call it alive, the energy is flowing. When something is broken, the heart is not pumping or anything or an essential thing in body is not functioning, then the body is called dead.

Q: Yeah that's how I know it...

K: Do you call your computer alive when it's running? And when it's not running do you cry that it's dead?

This whole block is all vibrations and the vibration of this [pointing to the body] is just an information of form, which is just kept together by the information. If that gets broken by another information, then it's a broken information, but that what is vibrating is not different in nature. The way it is vibrating is different – that's all.

Q [Another visitor]: The energy of the stone is not the same as the energy of the tree or the ground or the body absorbing energy...

K: It's all energy in different vibrations. You think there are different objects with energy – that's bullshit. This is all energy in vibration, this is light in vibration. So what is sucking what? The sucker is the same energy as the sucked.

Q [Another visitor]: The body is vibration of energy that has a given an information of form...

K: Yeah and when this vibration is not functioning anymore, the vibration collapses and naturally goes to the 'I Amness'. Energy cannot get lost.

Q [Another visitor]: So is there a vibration that gives life to a body?

K: It does not give life to anything. The energy in that vibration that you call life, it doesn't give any life. That what is energy – is life and it doesn't give any life to anything. It just shows itself as That, but it doesn't give any life to anything. Life cannot be given or taken away.

Q [Another visitor]: So when this body decomposes, some of them turn to different variety of microbes and some turn to gases...

K: Yeah. So don't burn yourself, don't be stingy, give yourself to the worms. They have a party after you die. A big party! Who cares what happens with that what is in vibration and then changes into something else? Transforming and transforming – in this relative transformation.

Q: With death does the idea of phantom the disappear?

K: No. The phantom is still there, the spirit is still there. It does not disappear, the perceiver is still there – as perceived. The experience of a perceiver is still there, which is not – That. It just shifts from the body thing to the space. That's why as per the Tibetan book of the dead, someone sits for forty eight days saying 'Don't go back into that information system. Stay where you are'. Otherwise you immediately jump into the next. This energy has total tendency of jumping into – where there are two liquids meeting and then something else is created again.

Q [Another visitor]: But does it help? The Tibetan technique...

K: It's a nice show.

Q: But does it help?

K: Yeah. To stay in the I Amness.

Q [Another visitor]: So the perception is still there but the experiencing of the phantom disappears?

K: No. The ownership of the body shifts from the 'I Am the body' to 'I Am Spirit'. The ownership shifts. Now you think you are this body – identified. Then you identify with the spirit, the identification shifts from being identified with the gross body to being identified with the space body. Then maybe the Tibetan book of the dead comes – talk to you and say 'Don't go back to the gross body'. Then by that you may have an opportunity to go one step further.

Q: To the first [awareness]?

K: Yeah.

Q: And then there is no experiencing of the phantom?

K: There is an experience of silence. Because that is light in its nature – silent and from there on, the tendencies that you want to go back, get burnt out.

Q [Another visitor]: Didn't you say we always come back?

K: Yeah, sooner or later, but you can go infinite times from there to there again. But someday someone will be sitting on your bed so that you go one step further.

Q: But still you can come back...

K: Even from there you can come back. If that tendency is really not annihilated, you will come back here. The Taoists are very clear. You can have thousands of years of *samadhi* of light, you always come back here. Because it is still one too many – this light experience.

Q [Another visitor]: Even if it's not connected to any particular form of a body?

K: No. It's still identified to light. There is God identified to the purest knowledge of existence as light. There is still God identified. As a purest notion, but the purest notion is still a notion of light. The notion of notionlessness. The notion, the no-notion and then *Om*, the purest light and sound experience. The purest of the purest is awareness – just being awake, that awakeness.

Q: So there is a tendency in that vibration to get denser...

K: This creator tendency is still there. The creator can always start creating, as spirit and what can be created. Whether this goes to the fourth [states of consciousness] is not certain. It is all by accident in a way – random.

Q [Another visitor]: And there still something happens?

K: No. Nothing happens from there. From there, there is no one identified anymore. There is no God who knows himself. God being That and That is not different. Even in that God doesn't know himself. In the first three, God knows himself as awareness, I Amness and the world. God knowing himself is a relative God.

God, in an absolute absence of any idea of God, is That what is God and from there, no God wakes up. There is no one who knows himself, in four, five, six and seven [state of consciousness]. There is no 'Knowing God' that knows himself as anything. He is That what is Heart that doesn't know any Heart. But in the first three, there is a God who knows himself. Knowing himself as awareness, knowing himself as spirit and knowing himself as body. These are the relative gods. The relative God who knows...

Q: From there [beyond the third state of consciousness], there is no coming back in the relative body?

K: From there nothing ever comes. There is no relative body here that can come in any body.

Q: In the Tibetan book of dead...

K: Goes from here to there.

Q: Okay...

K: God started to know himself and became a creator and from being the creator he started to create a spirit and then it becomes something what is created. He was dumb enough to wake up by waking up. Then he was dumber spirit and he was the dumbest – being dumped in this body experience and by taking himself as a so-called born body. Then even the unborn spirit is an identified God and even the awareness. So all that is identification.

Q: So if the identification is totally gone...

K: It's not a going of the identification, the identifier is gone. Because there was never any identifier – no definer.

Q [Another visitor]: When the Tibetans sit by the dead person, the vibration information changes to the 'I Amness' by their chanting. Then that can facilitate the change...

K: First you get established in the spirit. It's like Nisargadatta says, by 'who am I', get established in I Amness and from there on he has to go further. That was the first step, by the grace of his guru, by believing in him, he went from the identified body to being identified with spirit. From there, he even drops that – sooner or later and then you become identified with awareness. Then even that has to be dropped in a way.

Who drops the dropper? Because already there is a dropper that dropped the first two, but who drops the dropper? That happens only by grace. When grace is there, it will happen – the total. Then grace is there without knowing any grace – being grace. From grace, nothing ever happened anyway. Grace is what makes the difference. Manifested or non-manifested you are that what-is. That what is manifested, manifested. That what is non-manifested, non-manifested.

But right now you are manifested only in this body, different to other bodies. That is quite a difference and from there comes the Tibetan book of the dead. From there it leads you to the way back. The way back is from lowest, the middle and then the highest. From the highest, to be the highest – not knowing any highest. Because the highest doesn't know any highest becomes the middle who doesn't know any middle and then the lowest who doesn't know any lowest. Because it doesn't even know itself.

God not knowing himself, he is awareness, he is I Amness and he is the world and there is no difference in it. This is the end of separation but in all the first three, there is separation. But the way back is like you come out. You come back from the unknown to someone who is knowing himself. God knows himself – God oh God! Then he becomes out of that a lover and by loving, he comes from unknown to someone who knows himself. God knows himself – God oh God! Then he becomes out of that a lover and by loving, he creates a beloved – in his love affair.

And how to get out of that love affair? How to break this hypnotic love affair with yourself? First you drop the beloved, then only loving happens – loving as oneness. Then you see that even loving is not it. Then you remain as the lover himself, being the origin himself, but from there, you can start again.

So by grace alone – not even God can help himself, he just ceases away in to the total black sun – which never knows the sun – it's being the sun. The black sun is the sun, not knowing any sun. From the black sun, only what-is, the sun-is and whatever-is – is That.

You go astray first, by going in as one who can go astray and losing yourself. This is really the lowest of the lowest. Then you suffer that you know yourself. But the suffering starts already here [raising the thumb], the sufferer. Very early, that's the 'I' thought, the first card that Ramana speaks of. That where everything starts. God knowing himself, being aware to exist. The awareness of the existence, that is the beginning and the end of the relative experiencing and there the sufferer starts, not even suffering. But there already is a potential of suffering – sufferer, suffering, creating all that – look at it!

Q [Another visitor]: So where does the devoting the devoter coming into that?

K: By Grace. Grace is devoting the devoter, renouncing the renouncer – being what-you-are. Just by being what-you-are, which absolutely doesn't know itself. The absolute absence of any idea of what-you-are and what-you-are-not – your very nature.

Simply by being That, what-you-cannot-not-be, this is renunciation of the renouncer. The dropping of the dropper and nothing else can drop the dropper as you being what-you-are – in nature. The rest is the rest. It cannot give you the rest of what-you-are. The whole restaurant of the world, of light and spirit cannot give you the rest you are looking for. But it seems like, first, second, third and – [makes a popping sound]. From there, no one comes back, as no one came out of That in the beginning. There was never anyone who came out of it.

I say consciousness always knows best. If it creates the Tibetan or the Egyptian book of the dead, it always creates some tools of getting rid again from this relative tra...la...la... And it is always what is needed. Maybe, you are not for nothing born into a Christian circumstance.

Q [Another visitor]: It's interesting that when people die in hospitals, the people who are closest to them, leave the whole room. Even UG asked everybody to leave...

K: Yeah. You live in the memory of the closest, the memory is alive. It's like the energy of the memory keeps that alive. Just the perception of looking at that, keeps it there. The perception is creating and perception is like seer, giving energy to that what is being looked at. So when everyone goes, then it can dissolve. It's like you fix it there. You cannot let it go if you're fixed on it. You really fix the energy in that body by your energy with your eyes and memory because of your love. This love energy keeps it alive in that. So when this relative goes out, then it can subside.

Q [Another visitor]: It's best to live a life that I can get rid of, so that I don't get stuck to the love affair when I die...

K: [Asking another visitor] Did you understand what she said?

Q [Another visitor]: If you lead a life you don't love, then it's easier to get rid of it...

K: So kill your beloved before you go. Nothing works.

Q [Another visitor]: I was afraid so...

Q [Another visitor]: What about the theory of *karma*. That you're re-born according to what you've gathered in this life, you get the benefits in the next...

K: Yes you will. But not 'you' – consciousness, yes. Consciousness is the only thing that is incarnated here. There is no personal *karma*. The belief of personal *karma* is bullshit. But consciousness incarnated here is okay and will always have a wish for the next incarnation. There is no way out.

So there is infinite incarnation or *karma* of consciousness – action, reaction of one information transforming into something else. Action-reaction, infinite relating, never ending story of *karma* of consciousness.

Q: In other words, if you are born a king and you do good, in next life consciousness is born as something else...

K: Yeah, could happen – but don't take it personal. If you die, don't take it personal. [Laugher] That's all I can only say. Even now, don't take it personal, but who can do that? But if you could do that, not taking it personal, that would mean you are holy – already. But maybe even that is too much.

In my case, I take everything absolutely personal. By being consciousness, by being incarnated or not incarnated, there will never be any end of incarnation – of what I Am. Incarnating again and again and no end of that incarnation. Who cares of how it will be or not? It will always be the never ending story of consciousness and I Am That.

So, what is there to gain by the next or to lose? That's the main thing. There is nothing to gain or to lose in how it will happen next. No gaining or losing for what I am and whatever, but if you take it personal, then you may have to act now for what you want to prevent in the next. You have to earn the merits.

So, if you believe that you don't want to be reincarnated, just with the wish of not being re-incarnated anymore, you are already incarnated. Because that makes you incarnated now as a 'me' and by not wanting to re-incarnate again, you are already incarnated – as the next 'me'. Never ending story.

So, how to stop this? Again, the only way to stop this personal identification in whatever way, is being what-is. It's a full stop, because in that nothing ever happens. Nothing ever happened before, so it's not something new. It's an absolute full stopping as what-you-are which never moved. In all that movement, no one or nothing was moving in anything. Dream-like movements, never created any dream-like information. All the information of vibrations are – empty, that's the emptiness.

The easiest what you cannot do to stop the wheel of re-incarnation, is simply by being that wheel itself and not being the center. It's more like they want you to be the center because in center there is silence and everything is moving around you but you are not moving. It sounds always good and you're always attracted to that to be that – eye of the cyclone. [Mocking] Everything is moving around 'me' but 'I' am as calm as I can be – silence itself. But everything is moving, projecting around me – sounds good.

But then there will be a tendency that will pull you out again and it will leave you in the wind again.

Q [Another visitor]: So, if I don't want to re-incarnate, I would put the tendency to the one who is incarnated...

K: You are already incarnated again. [Laughter]

Q: By the vibration of that thought?

K: Yeah. The thought would re-incarnate again because that energy would get into the next. Any wish gets fulfilled – that's the problem with consciousness.

Q [Another visitor]: If I think of not getting re-incarnated at twenty, thirty and then again forty, do I create four lives?

K: At the end of your so-called bull-shit life, when you are so concentrated not to come back again, that wish is still there and by that wish you incarnate again. Don't take it personal, now this was twenty, thirty and forty – this guy. Fuck you!

Q: Thank you... [Laughter]

K: He really takes it personal now. Will I not be re-incarnated when I was twenty or thirty? What to do with that guy?

Q: So many wishes have come up and also have disappeared again...

K: Because you don't want to re-incarnate, you re incarnate the next morning again. The next moment is your re-incarnation, that's the whole problem. If you don't want to be now, you don't want to be the next moment and you don't want to be the next moment. That's only because you don't want to be now. You want to avoid this now, so you will become the avoider of the next now. You don't have to wait for the next life.

Q [Another visitor, laughing]: I only want to be re-incarnated with you Karl...

K: With me?! [Laughter] How can that be done? [Joking] Only because I dress so sexy or after a while it becomes sexy. It's amazing. [Laughter]

That wish keeps this coming again and again. But who cares?

Q [Another visitor]: These wishes...

K: The wishes of the witches. I'm always surrounded by witches and sorcerers. Consciousness trying to charm itself – snake charmers sitting here and trying to charm themselves. Trying to be very charming and clever, to charm themselves and control themselves. All the charming is trying to control what one is, by trying to know oneself. You're all snake charmers in that sense.

Q [Another visitor]: If in all the seven billion cases, the vibration shift happens, consciousness will still come back again?

K: Yeah. It would not make a difference. The moment it wakes up, everything is as it was before. No difference. You can go to the absolute black sun and then it wakes up and creates just as it was before. It cannot be otherwise, absolutely creating what can be created or not created. From the absolute un-manifested to the manifested, manifested as That!

It's like the upanishads, see you again – next time. No way out!

Q [Another visitor]: So the relative movement will come again?

K: It doesn't come again, it's never coming, never going. [Laughter] You will come again and again, with and without 'you'. So what?

Q: Absolute yes!

K: This is already a total *deja vu* of that movement; infinite times you experienced yourself the same before and you will again and again. Because this never comes and never goes, in that sense and is never changing.

February 12, 2009
Coimbatore

WHEN 'YOU' ARE – YOU ARE SHIT

Q: Are all the mythological stories fragmentation of the mind?

K: It's all a psychological explanation of how you are, how *Shiva* works in you. I'm just pointing out that it's all the nature of the Self – different tendencies, patterns of *Shiva*. So, even when *Shiva* gets married, he gets jealous like you. In the Bible, there are similar stories of God getting jealous and having revenge. It's everywhere. It's just a pointer to the Self in its different facets of experiencing itself. So, even God himself is not safe. If he exists, he gets the same bullshit as everybody. No way out.

Q: Sometimes you hear people say, I had never known or been conditioned into experience of *Kali* or *Shiva*, but it came to me. How does this happen?

K: It's like ancestors coming back. It's like you already had the knowledge buried in something and then the gate opens and the dead spirits wake up again. Everyone has these ancestors inside. Everyone is Indian, everyone is American, everyone is everything.

That's why people who go to India say, I feel at home, now I went back to where I belong. There are some parts in them that recognize the what was before, which was already there. So many stories. What comes up and pops up from this machine. It's all genetic tra... la...la. From the first *lingam* eruption, the whole Milky Way and every little cell in your body comes from That. All this information – stories, infinite stories. It's like a self-storage expressing itself in a unique way of what was before.

And then one takes it personal for what maybe your grandfather or grandma did. The emotion from the left and the emotion from the right, you never know where it comes from – how you react and why you react to something differently. Most of the times, you are able to explain it by saying my father was like this or my mother was like this, now I know why I'm like that. It must be running in your family.

If it's not in your father, then it must be somewhere before. But it doesn't matter where it comes from, it's not you. That's the main thing. It doesn't belong to you. It's just a result of all the events before. All what happened before, it's now like a cluster of little tendencies, what we call 'me' – personal story. And as much you want to solve it, as much you are involved and that is maybe the tendency of whatever you don't know why.

And that is the joke. You want to solve problems, which are not even yours. You want to get rid of the tendencies, which are not your tendencies. They all belong to this body and the body came from other bodies.

[A visitor coughs]

Her tendency of coughing is not there – it's just from a beast from before. The virus is even a tendency of – you don't know where it comes from. A mixture from all the diseases around you. Then maybe you would say next time I take care by not going there because I caught the virus there. Then you catch another one. Maybe it's even worse. Maybe the biggest virus is 'I am healthy'.

So all the organic food and health stuff is trying to avoid the tendencies and family constipation [mocking family constellation therapy] is like trying to clean up your family story, but that can go on forever. So it's all the story of *Shiva*. We're celebrating the marriage of *Shiva* and he could not avoid it.

As *Shiva* started to know himself, he created his wife – instantly. Parvati is everywhere, it's like space. *Lingam* and space and all what comes out of it, we just give it a name in different levels. The *yoni* is the impersonal space and Parvati is a personal space. It's like space – emptiness – no time. Then the *lingam*, which is the light of *Shiva*, vibrating in that space but in different levels. Out of That come all the different – five elements and the ether and the gross body and all what can be explained. All what *vedanta* tries to explain is – where does it comes from and what to do with it. It's all about different vibrations of light and different dimensions.

Q: What does *Kali* signify?

K: The destroying tendency of *Shiva*. They are just tendencies of *Shiva*. Parvati is the tendency of construction, constructing a family – like a family business. *Kali* is cutting down the family, chopping the heads and destroying whatever was created. Both the tendencies come out of *Shiva*.

Actually there is no family, there is only what-you-are. *Shiva* plays the father and the spirit. In Christianity it would be the father and the spirit and both together create the son. So it's all a way you realize yourself and *Kali* is the tendency to destroy the whole universe. Shiva-*Shakti*, *shakti* is the energy of *Shiva*. All different gods are just different tendencies of the absolute. Just having different names so that you can understand the nature of it – by giving it a form like a personal God. Just for making it a good story.

It's like a fairy tale, you have to give names. In Germany we have different names and they mean something else too – different tendency. I never tried to get another name because Karl means free man – one who doesn't have to bow down to anyone. That was fine with me and then that vibrates in you and maybe you behave like one. You never bow down or obey to anyone's wish.

In India they try to give you the vibration of that Indian name. They just see some tendency in you and they want to balance it by giving you a name of the balancing tendency. If you have too much war in you, they give you a name – shanti. All the people in India I know with the name shanti are the biggest fighters. They fight with everybody.

So, the masters try to balance the person. They become psychotherapists by just giving a name – fantastic! It's always an opposite. Then you wonder why does this guy have that name? It's all trying to explain what doesn't need to be explained. It's all family business – trying to balance something that doesn't need to be balanced and it's fun. Ramana never gave names, Nisargadatta never gave names.

There are teachers and psychotherapist masters who give names – like Osho and some others. There are traditions like Papaji, they all give names too. It runs through the lineage. But if you are in that tendency of Nisargadatta, it stops all lineages and names because you know that whatever name you give is – bullshit.

Q [Another visitor]: You also give names. Shit, shit shit...

K: Yeah, but that's the most common name. [Laughter]

Q [Another visitor, mocking]: Because we're so beautiful inside, you need to give the opposite...

K: The inner shit is very soft. [Laughter] We can now make a story that *sadgurus* don't give names and *gurus* give names to – whatever. So, there is a little difference of what people talk about – the unpronounceable and the pronounceable. What can be pronounced, you give names and what cannot be pronounced, you just be quiet about That. Whatever you can name is shit in that way.

So you can make it easy, you can call everything shit. Just to make it easy. Then you don't have to remember. Then whoever you meet – Ah, shit! That's neither-neither. That's *neti-neti*, you meet the one who neither is, nor is-not. In the morning, the shit song starts. You're only in the universe because you give it names. But if you only have one name for everything, then there is no discrimination of anything. Sounds good but it doesn't help either – but one tries.

So, it's called 'shit'-sang. [Laughter]

Q [Another visitor]: Even the scientists agree that everything that you think in your senses, is bound to have a reaction...

K: Not always.

Q: Everything...

K: No reaction is another reaction, that's right.

Q: It seems like even they agree that everything is automatic...

K: It shows that there are infinite pearls of reactions that react to the totality. So, you cannot not react to what-you-are as you are That.

Q: Automatic...

K: It's the nature of consciousness reacting to itself – that's all there is. There is only reaction you can experience, the action – you cannot experience. The reactions reacting to reactions.

Q: And there is no end to it?

K: No. There is no way out of it. There is no better way of reacting to it and when I call it shit, I mean it. It's all shit reacting to shit. By trying to get out of the shit, you are in the shit. You cannot leave what-you-are because you are That – what is shit. But That what is shit, doesn't know any shit. That's why maybe it's not so bad to be shit. So, I recognize myself in everything, because I am shit. Shit...shit...shit.

If I call myself knowledge, I have to always knowledge myself and that's too much effort for me. Shit comes so naturally, I tell you.

Q [Another visitor]: What do you mean by – I recognize myself in everything?

K: By being shit, you're That – what-is. Then calling yourself as

That what-you-are, comes naturally. Shit...shit...shit – by being shit. Because what wakes up in the morning, whatever can say something, already is shit. It's already a relative experience of whatever is relative and experience of relative existence. So, already you're shit.

The experience of existence is already shit and then recognizing yourself as what-you-are as relative experiences – is shit...shit...shit. So, when I call it shit, it's just a self-recognition, Self recognizing itself. Because the Self that recognizes is already a shit. The recognizer, the recognizing and what can be recognized – is shit. Call it relative or not, I call it shit.

Q: So, waking up in the morning, the phantom is recognizing that it's in the...

K: The recognizer wakes up. The recognizer is shit. Just by being what is shit, already relative, whatever you say is shit. Whatever you say, whatever you do, whatever you see – is shit. From false, the false can only experience false. Shit can only experience shit. So, that becomes sat-'shit'-*ananda* – the happiness of shit.

Q: While all that is happening, there still is un-mentionable parallel of being-what-you-cannot-not-be...

K: What-you-are, you are inspite of that shit.

Q: There is no way that the relative can get to That, so how is it possible?

K: You realize yourself as shit, as you cannot realize yourself as real. Because reality can never be realized. Whatever you realize, the first you realize is the realizer. That is already – shit – discomfort. So the realizer is already relative to That what is realizing, so it's shit.

But that what is the reality of what-you-are, cannot be realized. So, the real never needs to be real. The one who realizes itself as whatever, can only realize itself as shit. So, it starts as shit...shit...shit. It's easy and in none of that, you can get lost or you can be found. Because the nature of shit is *chit* and the nature of even the relative shit is *chit*.

Q: So, that which seems to be...

K: Is also shit and then you want to get out of shit, that makes you feel shit. Then you really feel shitty, because you are in shit. But when you are already shit when you wake up, when shit is there – as 'you' – then what you experience, is not different than what-you-are. Then there is shit...shit...shit.

And no way out of shit. It starts already with shit and whatever follows after that can only be shit. The relative seer, can only see relative, what can be seen, but it will never be real. So, it's shit...shit...shit. It's actually quite a joy – the joy of shit or peace of shit. Because there is no expectation in the next moment, as if that the next moment can be less shit.

Q: So, it's like a recognition of the conscience...

K: It's a recognition that what was shit, is shit and whatever will come will be shit. Shit...shit...shit. It starts with shit and the moment 'I Am' – it's shit. Whatever then comes from that existence to-be – is shit. Whatever comes! And whatever comes and goes is shit. So what?

I'm talking about peace. I'm talking about the peace of shit and anything else, if you take one thing out of it and make it special, you really feel shitty. Because then, you really experience shit. Then you, as an experiencer, are different to that what is shit. Then you take yourself as an arrogant, better than shit. Then you become the little devil, who wants to decide what is shit and what is not shit. By thinking what-is and what-is-not shit, you are in the discrimination bullshit. Then you suffer about discrimination.

That's the suffering – that you think, something is not shit. That you're maybe expecting in the future, there is a moment that is not shit. That you call enlightenment and if there is in future a possibility of enlightenment, this moment really stinks. But only because there is future moment of not stinking. It will always stink.

What to do? By instinct – it stinks.

And even the not stinking, stinks. Because the stinker is there – which is 'me'. Everything stinks because the relative experiencer is there, with a relative existence. Whatever happens from there on – stinks. It's all relative experiences and they always will be – shit. More or less shit, but it will always be shit. More or less discomfort, more or less misery. So what?

Misery means experience of separation. You cannot stop it. That's called 'me'-sery [misery]. Where there is a 'me', there is a me-sery and you will always miss yourself and that's an experience of shit. The one who misses himself, even as a potential 'misser', is a potential shit.

Q: So what you're suggesting is to surrendering to the shit?

K: Don't surrender, just be-what-you-cannot-not-be. Because the moment you wake up, you're shit. I'm talking about what-you-cannot-not-be – a relative experiencer.

Q: Bringing it into the relative...

K: You can only experience yourself relatively. Even the experience of 'I' is a relative experience. So, it starts with shit. So, be-what-you-cannot-not-be means that you're already shit and trying not to be shit... [Laughing mockingly]

That what is the nature of nature never needs to be anything. But the moment you experience yourself, you cannot not be shit. Because you can only be in the relative experience. So, be-what-you-cannot-not-be is shit and whatever comes from there – is shit. Ramana called it false, the experience of 'I'. The false waking up and out of the false, only false follows. Whatever comes from the false is false. False, false, false. So, even right is false.

I call it shit, because for me it comes more naturally. That's all. I can call it false, false, false. But then I have to make a little effort. Shit is more fun for me. False, false, false is too serious. I'm not so serious and that's why I like UG Krishnamurthy, he was also in the same fun business. In that way, I'm not different from Ramana or Nisargadatta, whatever they said. But there are tendencies which come naturally and for this farmer's son, shit comes naturally.

Otherwise you will have to call it the first relative experience, from the first relative experience now. Then the next relative experience following – it already becomes a heavy teaching. Shit, shit, shit is very light. So, I'm very delighted by shit – very light. [Laughter] That's the joy of shit and peace of shit and the knowledge of shit. Any experience compared to what-you-are is shit. Even being what-you-are – is shit.

Q: What do you mean by being what-you-are?

K: Even by being what-you-are, there is one who is, what one is – it's shit. So, even if you are the Self, it's shit. Already by being the Self, is shit. It's fun, I tell you. You're the shit of the shit. You can make a story of an absolute ass, experiencing itself as an absolute ass-hole – already you feel like shit. Because you know, shit will come – sooner or later [Laughter]

Every relative experience, experiencing yourself as an ass, is experiencing yourself as an ass-hole and for sure sooner or later, shit happens. You know it. Even as a clean ass-hole, you know, you will be dirty again. Even being an awareness ass-hole, an ass-hole of light, you know – shit happens. The *prana* ass-holes, the pure ass-holes. I like these organic, esoteric ass-holes, trying to become clean.

Maybe they even meant *sat-shit-ananda*. That sat is shit and that is joy and the moment sat is, Self is – it's shit.

Q [Another visitor]: You will be known as a shit guru...

K: That is already UG Krishnamurti. It's all stolen anyway. If you call it false, it's stolen from Ramana, if you call it shit, you steal it from UG. Even UG stole it from Ramakrishna [Paramhansa]. Nothing is original, thank God. And you don't have to worry about if you're original or not. Because that's the biggest shit you want to be in – the original shit. It's the biggest bullshit, trying to become origin of everything.

But then who wants to become the origin of shit? That's quite relaxing because even being origin is shit. [Laughter] But if you're the origin of truth, the origin of freedom and truth, all your precious bullshit, then you already want to share it with everybody. But if you're the origin of shit, maybe you don't tell everybody. [Laughter]

Everybody says I'm the embodiment of truth, but if you say I'm the embodiment of shit [Laughter] – shit actually feels, not so bad. That's your nature anyway – feeling shitty – the moment you exist, you feel shitty. If you can only experience shit, it's a peace of shit.

Q [Another visitor]: If you start thinking as everything is shit...

K: You don't have to think it, you have to be it. You're already shit.

Q: But now I think I'm this body and that is not shit...

K: That's the reaction of shit. Paulo thinks he's a better shit, that's your problem, not our problem. There's the absolute advantage that in shit there is no advantage for anybody.

Q: When you say this, it gives a sense of freedom but that is still a way...

K: It's a piece of shit.

Q: But it makes me kind of...

K: Because you want to feel special, you feel miserable, but it's not my problem. So, enjoy your misery. From shit you want to make something better.

Q: But if I try to make everything as shit, I'm trying to change something everyday.

K: So what?

Q: So I need to make an effort there...

K: It's shit there and shit there. Both is shit. You have to make a fucking effort anyway and if you make effort, it's shit. The result will be shit. I can only present how it works here [pointing to himself]. I don't want to change anybody. If you are another way, I give a shit about it.

Q: I just ask, why do I feel that?

K: Now you're getting into that personal bull-shit again. This little Italian ass-hole wakes up and thinks that personal shit is more than the impersonal shit. You take your sword out and try to fight with bull-shit. If you don't feel it, then you're more ignorant than I think.

Q: What should I do?

K: Kill yourself. Do you think anyone gives a shit about it?

Q: Now you're going somewhere...

K: Yeah. Now I go to that shit. I give a shit about how one does something.

Q: It's only this shit reaction that makes me unhappy...

K: No one wants to make you happy. You have a taste and that's your problem. By having a taste, you already taste shit because you make differences. Making difference is shit and not making difference is shit. You cannot get out of it. So, if you're born and have a taste, it's shit, but what to do? You cannot go against it. Just see that it will be shit.

Every tendency, everything that makes a difference is shit and not making a difference is shit. I just point out to the indifference of shit. None of that will make you happy – nothing, not one of that. So, the moment you are, 'you-are' – it's shit. Whatever comes out of that being, out of existence – it produces shit. All relative concepts coming out of that first concept of existence.

What else do I point to? Don't say you will be happy. That's why I get angry because I say you'll never be happy and you expect that you'll get happy, by what I say. You go totally against what I say – since years! I say no one is here to make you happy, because you'll never be happy. There's no happiness which you can experience. But you say [in a whining tone] 'I cannot be happy' and then I say 'Fuck you! Go and kill yourself somewhere else. Who gives a shit?'

I say every moment 'you' can only experience misery but not 'what-you-are' – that's all. And still after fifteen years you say 'But I don't feel happy by that' and then I get a bit pushy.

Q: You've only started to shit in last few years, before that it was different...

K: I just called it differently – that's all. If this mechanic doesn't make you happy, go with your car somewhere else. [Laughter] Like it or leave it. It's like you go to a doctor and complain that the pills don't work. But the doctor tells you in advance that I cannot make you healthy, I cannot help you. I can give you pills and then you complain – that doesn't help. But he told you in the beginning, 'I cannot treat you'. There's nothing in for you here, but still you complain, 'I don't feel so well after your pills'.

Q [Another visitor]: Your pills are bitter...

K: Only the bitter medicines help. In Taoism they say – Beautiful words for sure cannot be true and the truth is never beautiful. So, to tell you that it will never be beautiful, there will never be a happy moment in your life is not a nice message – I know, but I have to tell you.

Q: And the art is not to take it as a medicine...

K: That's the ultimate medicine. That there's no one who is sick and no one can be treated. And whoever can be treated is a piece of shit already who wants to be healthy and enlightened and who gives a fucking shit about if a shit is enlightened or not? Only another shit. Only a shit is happy or unhappy. Who gives a shit about a happy shit or an unhappy shit?

Q: You cannot talk to the mind...

K: I don't want to talk to the fucking mind. Who wants to talk to the fucking mind?

Q: I can only listen to you as music...

K: What music? Whose bloody ears call something as music and something as not music?

Q: It's not in my control, it happens...

K: You see, shit happens!

Q: How many years have you tried and how many have succeeded in hearing you?

K: No one! No one ever! No one got it!

Q: When did you get it?

K: I never got anything! Shit happened!

Q: Then why are you not angry at him? [pointing at another visitor] [Laughter]

K: Now he fights for someone else, now he's more shit fighter.

Q: No one can get it, unless it happens by itself...

K: What will happen? [Laughter] Still there's hope that something will happen by itself. It's amazing! Now we have to start all over again.

Q: Yes. Everyday we start all over again. [Laughter] By talking nothing happens...

K: Awww... You started it and there will always be reaction to what-you-are and now you say nothing happened. There will be reaction whether you like it or not. When it pleases your concepts, you make it a different story – as everybody does.

Q: Yes! Including you!

K: I change my shirts every second and the nakedness is still the nakedness – with or without the shit story.

Q: Hopeless...

K: I know and that's why I call everyone around me 'hopeless cases', including this guy.[pointing to himself]; He's a hopeless case. I'm talking to hopeless cases, hopeless shit talking to hopeless shit and there is a peace of shit.

But any moment you hope that some moment may come and shit will realize shit, it will not be a different moment. There will still be shit realizing shit. So, nothing happens because it's not that something is changing – at all. Shit will realize shit. There was shit realizing shit before, there is shit realizing shit now and there will be shit realizing shit after that – what we call realization.

The realization will always be the realization, but it will never be the real, that what you imagine to be real. It will always be – relative. An experience of relative experiences of realization of what-you-are but never that what you're looking for – never ever. So, what to do?

Q [Another visitor]: I could never get enough of shit. [Laughter] Twenty years of smoking this shit!

K: You can never shit as much as you eat. The outcome is always shit. Whatever comes, whatever goes, whatever stays, whatever is and is-not – is always shit. You can call it shit or you can call it a concept, what difference does it make?

Q: So, you're saying whatever I imagine to get...

K: No! Even that is shit. You cannot forget yourself. You have to realize yourself, but you always have to realize yourself as shit.

Q: In whichever way...

K: In whatever way, it will be an experience of a relative way, of relative concepts of differences. You will never experience yourself in anything and whatever you experience is not what-you-are in that sense. Some call it reflection or realization, I call it shit – that's all. Just to make it easy for this guy [pointing to himself] otherwise

I have to use these words all the time.

Q: So, that would be the problem, I want to change something, I want to...

K: You want to make gold out of shit. You're the inner sorcerer, an alchemist who wants to make gold out of shit, but you cannot. Because that what is trying to make gold out of shit is already shit. So, shit wants to find gold. He wants to find himself because he thinks that he's gold.

And you're right, your nature is that gold, but you cannot find it in shit. You always look in the wrong place. Wherever you look, you can only find it in the wrong place but not what-you-are. But every night with the absolute absence of any presence of idea of shit or no-shit, you are what-you-are as you are here – what-you-are. But that never knows itself. That knowledge of what-you-are never knows or doesn't know anything. And That you can call it knowledge – call it *chit*.

Chit means knowledge. But whatever *chit* is experiencing, is not *chit* – it's shit and I can only point to That. It fits in the Indian tradition because *chit* is the name for knowledge – *jñana*. Whatever can be experienced – *jñani* – is already shit. In that way, the experience of *jñani*, is already a relative experience of That what is *jñana*. So, if a *jñani* knows a *jñani*, he knows himself as shit. The moment *jñani* knows himself, he knows shit. Every *jñani* who knows *jñani*, for sure is one *jñani* too many.

Q: And that is shit...

K: Because only shit can be known and only shit claims to know himself. That what is *jñana* will never claim to know itself – that never says anything. There is no claiming – never needs to claim anything.

The Real doesn't need to be real – to be real. It would never call itself real or not real. But whoever calls himself as real or truth, for sure is false. It has to be unreal and unreal is a different word for shit, for me. I just call it shit. I could call it unreal, concept or whatever. But for sure, it's not that what is nature of nature.

So, when nature knows nature, it's a false nature, it's an artificial nature. Any knowing where there is a knower is a relative knowledge and that is an artificial knowledge. It's a realization but not the reality. Reality will never call itself reality. There is not even a word for reality – for Reality. It will never pronounce itself. And that what pronounces itself – the relative pronouncer – can only pronounce whatever can be pronounced relatively, but never pronounces himself, but he tries.

But whatever he pronounces becomes shit because it's different from something else. Whatever is different to something else, is relative and shit to That – what doesn't even know to exist or not to exist.

Q: There is 'me' in the shit...

K: Even that is shit. There is no 'me' in shit. There is just shit, shit shit...

Q: Is it bound to be like that?

K: So what? Shit happens!

Q: Hopeless!

K: Failure! The absolute failure.

Q: I like that!

K: Failing, failing failing. I can have different words for it but shit comes most easily.

Q: But we were talking about you and then we make you into something again...

K: Do whatever you like. Both is shit. Not making it is shit and making it is shit. So, it's a freedom of shit.

Q [Another visitor]: No way out...

K: It's always like that. For whatever time you give special attention to that and then it goes away again. From the mystery it comes and back to the mystery it goes, but the mystery is still the mystery.

The moment I sit here and not expect to make someone happy, is not so bad. The moment I would sit here and expect that I can give you something, like an experience of happiness or I could please you or make you unhappy, I would be quite exhausted. Just by the idea, I'm already exhausted. Only with this idea, I can stay in bed forever. Going to these meetings and doing it twice a day!

That's why Eckhart Tolle has to rest a day by just giving a lecture, not even having an interaction. Already trying to teach that makes you so exhausted. Then expecting that a new earth comes from that, a new earth shit, you're absolutely exhausted. Then you have to hold hands with Dalai Lama day and night. [Laughter]

Q [Another visitor]: Give me some energy...

K: Give me some transmission or *diksha* or *shakti-pat*. I call it a shit transmission, a cheater transmitting a cheating energy to another cheater. [Mocking] I always think these *gurus* will send some assassins to kill me. Should I stop? No... too much fun, cannot stop.

Q [Another visitor]: So, trying to understand is shit and trying not to understand is also shit.

K: Yeah. It's quite relaxing. You cannot stop trying to understand it. Even trying to stop is that you're trying to understand it. Because someone told you that if you be quiet, it will come naturally.

Q: That's why I try to close my eyes...

K: It's an inner direction – the inner direction shit. Then you dig into the inner shit. Nisargadatta would say that the medicine is like everyone tried to find himself in the outer shit. Then you have to turn around to the inner shit to see that even in the inner shit, the inner direction, there is no where to find you! Neither in the outer or in the inner shit, you can find what-you-are. Because even the inner direction experience, the inner experience, is as shitty as the outer experience. And in that shit, you rest as that what never needs to rest. Because whatever you can find, will be shit.

Q: Or not find...

K: Now you claim that you can sit aside somewhere and 'not find'.

Q: I'm trying...

K: But even that is trying to find. Every moment you exist, you try to find a way out of existence. Inquiry will never stop.

It's not so bad – it's worse! Never ending shit story. Who can take that? No one! And what-you-are, never needs to take anything because it doesn't even know itself. So, there's no one who needs to take it, but the moment you exist, you want to take the shit. You can never take the shit. Even by understanding that there is no way out and there will be no ending of shit – no end of shit.

Q [Another visitor]: Now it's clear but when I go out...

K: You just make another concept out of it. That's why I don't say this is the end of the story. This just continues. Even out of that concept, you try to make it a better concept then the story before. But still the pointer for me is – be-what-you-cannot-not-be – because the moment you-are, it's shit. There is a relative experience of existence – that's shit.

So, be-what-you-cannot-not-be is being shit, because there is shit, shit, shit. But still every night in deep-deep sleep there is not even a presence of one who is or is-not. Then you're That – where there is no-shit. But the moment you know yourself, you experience yourself as shit and when there is no one, there is no shit. Shit and no-shit. You're in shit and you're in no-shit – what-you-are.

You even don't depend on the presence of shit – to be. You're in the shit experience and you're in the no-shit experience – what-you-are. So, you're shit and you're no-shit. But what-you-are, you will never know. You only know, when you're shit – you're shit;

when there's no-shit, you're no-shit. When there's presence, there is presence of a shit and when there's absence, there's an absence of a shit. So, you don't even have to be shit – to be what-you-are.

When you-are – you're shit. When you-are-not – you're not and maybe that's a pointer to That what is not a concept. That what is the Self, knowing the Self – is shit. Not knowing the Self is no-shit, but it cannot avoid knowing itself. So, it cannot avoid realizing itself. The moment it's realizing itself, it's realizing itself as shit. But every night not realizing itself – is *chit* because there is a knowledge without a knower.

But any moment you exist, you realize yourself as knower, knowing, what can be known. That is always realization of what-you-are but not That what-you-are in nature. But you can only realize yourself as shit.

Nothing to get here – even that is too much. What can be given, it comes out of one who gives something, it's a poison – gift. That what you can take is poison, but what to do? But that poison cannot kill you. So, who cares? But whatever can be given – is poison, but what-you-are cannot die because it was never alive. That what can die, is already dead.

The ultimate medicine – Being that, what is in dying not dying and in born, not born. You cannot avoid one experience. The experience of birth, you could not avoid. But as you're not born in that experience because prior to that experience you have to be, during and beyond.

So, nothing ever happened. It's just a pointer that shit happens, but in that shit happening – what to do?

I can only point to that helplessness. You cannot avoid as a shit. You cannot avoid knowing yourself, but any moment you know yourself, it's an experience of unhappiness – you cannot avoid it. You cannot avoid the misery. You can only realize yourself in misery and you have to realize yourself. You're that what has to realize itself – if you like it or not.

And I agree, the moment you realize yourself – you're relative and you cannot avoid having that relative experience. But by that relative experience, it doesn't make you relative – that's all I can point to. All you can experience – is shit. But that what is experiencing itself as shit, as first experience of 'I' – never knows itself as anything. It will never know itself, but it can only know itself as shit and it will always be there. No way out of realization.

So, what did Nisargadatta point to? You always have to realize yourself. But for sure, the shit takes it personal and says 'I have to realize myself'. So, I'm looking in a special way. It cannot be something I don't like. It has to be something that I like, whatever is pleasant, whatever is comfortable. So, you make it a concept.

No! You have to always realize yourself in the misery of life. And I sit here and say – be happy about it. Be happy, that you can never be happy and will never become happy. Because if you could experience happiness, you would be different from it. If it would be a different experience, a relative experience, then that happiness would be a relative happiness. But it would never satisfy you. You would never be satisfied by a relative experience.

So, temporarily there will be a relative peace of – whatever, but what comes will be gone again – you know that. It's just a little pause and pauses are like being in the oneness or in the awareness. Then you have like little breaks from misery, but the misery waits for you – again and again. You cannot avoid it. Temporarily, by whatever effort, you get out of that – by understanding, by whatever, deep insights, profound resting. All these *vedanta* techniques can give you temporary breaks, but this waits for you – if you like it or not.

The Taoists are very clear. You can go into the thousands and thousands of years of *samadhi* of light – but this market place waits for you. If you come back, and sooner or later you will come back, you are as thirsty as before and the misery waits for you – if you like it or not. And if you cannot be in the misery of this moment and this thirst of what-you-are, you will never become it, in any other place. This is one absolute aspect of your absolute realization. This moment of so-called relative misery.

So, all the absolute differences, by effort can be reached. But whatever you can reach by effort – this waits for you! The moment the effort is out of it, because it's not your effort, you end up here again. In this – whatever you call it. I call it shit.

Q: And praise the Lord!

K: Praise the Lord – just-in-case. I don't know who I Am, but this is not what I Am, because if I would be what I Am, I would be comfortable. It would be comfortable to be what I Am and if I would be home, it would be the comfort of being home. So, this cannot be my home. Then you look for home.

Q: Yesterday I was listening to Jiddu Krishnamurti and he asked the people who visited him – why do you want this light? Just tell me why do you want that?

K: I can tell you why you want this light because any moment you're Paulo, it's misery and the light is just the idea of the end of misery.

Q: Inside me there was a question, why am I looking for that?

K: The whole universe looks for happiness. Why should you be any different?

Q: I was looking inside for something more, to find the solution of this question. I was trying to stay in there and find the solution...

K: That's why he gave you that question. UG [Krishnamurti] always gave the question – try to find your original question. Then you try and try and you cannot find it, as you don't even know why you're looking for yourself? It's a second-hand information, someone told you something, you read something and maybe you think that it sounds good, there must be something because you always miss something. You don't even know what.

But then someone gives it a name – that's all. They call it enlightenment or happiness or being content or peace. It's a second hand information, you give a name to something you miss, but you don't even know what you miss. And I sit here and tell you – be happy that you miss what-you-are in every moment because if you would be something what you cannot miss, because it's there, you would be something what comes and goes. Be happy that you're always that what is being missed – never can be found in anything. The notion of missing will not stop.

And you take it as something negative, for me it's the absolute positive. That you always miss yourself in everything. Even missing yourself in the misser, you miss yourself. That you cannot be found in anyone or anything. Not in any experience, you can find yourself. But you take it as negative and that makes you a seeker. That makes it miserable. But seeing that there is a joy of missing yourself, because what you are can never be known.

Q: This I know, but...

K: There is no 'but' in it. There is only a but if there is one who takes it as negative.

Q: Yeah...

K: And that's 'me'. He always makes shit out of everything.

Q: For me, this is not so bad...

K: It's worse. The fucking one who has to tell that his life is not so bad, is a fucking ass-hole right away. [Laughter] You may rot in hell forever – no one gives a damn.

Q: So why I'm looking for that? As soon as I was finished, I started to look again. I said, no, yes, no...

K: Yes, no, yes, no – that's called milking a cow. Opening, closing, opening, closing – milking yourself.

Q: I asked the same question last year... [Laughter]

K: And the year before.

Q: Is it quite nice to be what-you-are?

K: No. It's the sweetness itself. It's beyond the relative taste of sweetness and it's sweetness itself.

Q: But nobody knows…

K: But I Am That.

Q: Is it not possible to have that in relative?

K: No. You're That or you're not. When you're not, you're in the misery of not being That. When you are That, there was never any misery.

Q: This is another problem. I know this, it's clear, but…

K: But because you want to have it, you miss it – and that's the misery. You're greedy and that makes you miserable and you cannot stop the greed because you're helpless in that. The greed is there – no way out. The loving, caring and greed for yourself, you cannot stop. You don't even know what you're greedy for. And everyone gives different names for that. [Joking] You go to Mooji, maybe he'll give you something.

Q: No, I'll have to start all over again and remember the vocabulary there… [Laughter]

K: I'm easy, shit is easy.

Q: No. You're not very easy, I tell you. [Laughter]

K [Asking another visitor]: Am I easy?

Q [Another visitor]: When I hear that it is easy, when I turn around, it's not so easy.

K: But it's easy not to be easy for you. It's easy not to be easy. You don't need any effort to make problems. It's very easy.

Q: I have a tendency to make it not easy…

K: It's not a tendency – you don't have any tendency. It's just your fucking nature – the fucker has to fuck. The mind has to mind the mind. What to do with it? The relative will always mind the relative. What can the relative do? What can the God who knows himself do about himself? He has to care about himself. The God becomes mind. God knowing God is already mind. God becomes mind and the nature of mind is minding the mind. What else can it do?

And you cannot stop it, because only in separation you can realize yourself – that's mind. Mind means two and there is no other way of realizing yourself. There will never be any end of the experience of two – it never started. Because you realize yourself even there – no way out. You have to be inspite of That – what-you-are, because it will never end. You cannot end the realization of what-you-are and you will always realize yourself in separation. There is no other way. The dream of realization will always be the dream of separation. No beginning, no end.

And as infinite, as the nature of life, is life living life. But life can only live life in the experience of one, two, three – father, spirit, son. Call it whatever – *Shiva* and *shakti* – already two. *Shiva* and the light of *Shiva* – already two. You cannot live with or without you. You cannot live with you and you cannot live without you.

Q: Does your reaction comes from [pointing his thumb] this?

K: It's always different. It comes from there, where it comes from. There is no one there, who defines there what is better. If it's a body reaction, it's a body reaction. If it's the space reacting, it's the space reacting. If it's That, then it's That. For me there's no difference in nature. If I react personally, it's same as impersonal.

That's why I say, the shit reacts and shit always has differences of shit. The difference of shit between the personal shit and the impersonal shit and even that beyond shit. Shit, shit, shit. And only that shit reacts, because reactions are only reactions of action, but action never reacts to anything. Only in the realization there are differences of reactions from different reference points. But in the Absolute – that what is That – it's absolutely indifferent on how it reacts. It makes no difference.

Q: For what I Am?

K: For the nature it makes no difference.

Q: When you talk, you sometimes say that I don't talk to you...

K: But even if I talk to the relative ass-hole Paulo, I talk to myself. I always talk to myself. I don't make a different talking to the ass-hole or the ass. It's both not different in nature. So, even if it's personal, I talk to myself. Then you make it a personal self reaction and impersonal self reaction and then even beyond. It makes no difference. I can only talk to myself – in whatever way.

I don't talk to that. I don't make [pointing his thumb] this as more Self than that [pointing his middle finger] Self – no more or less Self. I talk to the ass-hole Paulo.

Q: The energy thinks that it's the ass-hole Paulo...

K: Doesn't matter. The energy never thinks. Now you make energy, shit, as if energy could think. The vibration of the energy, you call the thinker is thinking what can be thought. But all of that, in nature, is energy and energy is never thinking. The energy is vibrating as a thinker, thinking what can be thought but is never thinking.

Q: Can you tell again?

K: No. [Laughter] The energy is always vibrating differently, but energy is never reacting. Only the vibration of energy is vibrating to another vibration of energy. But That what is the vibration is never reacting to anything. There is silence – the silence of whatever is there, vibrating as whatever, but never reacting to another silence and that is energy. What you're talking about is already a relative shit – relative energy. Fuck it!

I like that. I can be personal as shit and I still talk to myself and I can be impersonal and I talk to myself. The energy is vibrating here as a talker and there as a listener. This talker is sometimes talking personal and sometimes impersonal to that what is sometimes personal and sometimes impersonal. But that, what is vibrating there and here in nature, is absolutely no different. It can be absolutely personal or absolutely impersonal, it makes no difference. Who gives a shit about it? Who says one is better than the other? 'Me' That really makes it shit.

Q: Yeah, but I really need some gain...

K: Just-in-case.

Q [Another visitor]: Often people say, I feel the energy of *Shiva*...

K: Already a lie. How can you feel the energy of *Shiva*? You can experience vibration, reactions, call it whatever, you will never experience *Shiva*. If you experience *Shiva*, you're dead. You can only experience *Shiva* when there is no one who is experiencing *Shiva*. But even having an idea of what is and what is-not *Shiva*, who can experience that? Crazy!

[Mocking] Oh, today there's more *Shiva* energy than yesterday, sounds good – that's all. It means that you have some discrimination, you make a diary of *Shiva*'s energy. But still we can talk about it. The *Shivaratri* is the absence of the presence of the absence, presence. You're the energy but you don't feel it anymore – blah, blah, blah...

One gets more and more confused and still one-is. The best you can say is, I have no idea what Karl was talking about. I enjoy it, but I don't know why. That's the best one can say. Because then you don't have to remember why and you're not longing to go back. Always to be in enjoying it but don't know why.

Q [Another visitor]: There were times when I never wanted to leave this place, but now it's okay...

K: But that's the nature of joy, that you can even enjoy going. Because you have nothing to miss there. That's what I'm talking about. It's very nice because you don't have to stay. You may stay or you don't stay, but both is okay or not. Who cares? That's what

The Song of Irrelevance

I like. It's the same shit here as anywhere else. [Laughter] So you're here or you're there, you enjoy the shit because it will never stop.

In Germany there's a city where they say, somewhere else is as shitty as here. They just know it because they live in the most shitty place. So, what to do? I'd rather be here, if I cannot leave it. If you go to the most distant place in the universe, because 'you' are there, shit is there. [Laughter]

I mean it, wherever 'you' are, it's shit because 'you' are there. So, be-what-you-cannot-not-be means – you're shit. So, what? And wherever you are, there will be shit and it will not stop. Wherever you are is shit, there is no discrimination anymore because it was, it is and it will be – shit. Because wherever you are, there is shit. For sure! You go to the best place on this planet. You have a five star awareness club, everything is fine. But because you are there – it's shit. It's the most perfect place on this earth but because 'you' are there – it's shit.

That's barren bay, very nice, very beautiful but because 'you' are there – it's shit and you go to whatever, it's shit. Normally the 'me' means that grass is always greener somewhere else. You expect that if I go there, than I will be happy then here. But I tell you, you will be there. Because you will be there, it will be as shit as here. Because you have to take yourself there too.

And wherever there is a 'me', there is a misery, if you like it or not. So what? So, better enjoy yourself in the misery because the misery will never stop. Because you cannot realize yourself without the 'me'. The phantom, you cannot kill because that what is killing the phantom, is itself a phantom. Even the phantom who kills the phantom, is still a phantom who kills the phantom. And wherever the phantom is, there is shit.

So, that's why they say, if a *jñani* by whatever understanding still knows himself as a *jñani*, he knows himself as shit. So, even that is shit. So, even enlightenment is shit, because there is one who is enlightened, it's a shit of enlightenment. Or an awakened shit. [Laughing mockingly] Look there is awakened shit. Then one awakened shit talks to another unawakened shit – 'You should wake up because being awakened shit is better shit'.

That happens and when I say only shit happens and shit talks and shit talks to shit. This is shit talk. And I'm pointing out that because of that talking, you cannot get out of the shit. Because whoever is listening here, wants to get rid of that listener. But you cannot get rid of it. That's why it's called a fun-tom. You better have fun with yourself because without the phantom, there is no Self. Fantastic! It's all fantasy!

It's always bad when you get what you like, but the opposite is equally bad. [Laughter] It's like black and white *tantra*. Aleister Crowley would say it's better to get what you don't like because it's easier to let go again. But it's just the same shit because you start that and you fall in love with that. Because you fall in love with the idea of it and then if something goes wrong, it really goes wrong. It's like arranged marriages, suddenly they fall in love.

Existence has fun, I tell you. Especially if someone tries to control something. [Laughing mockingly] But not controlling is the same – then you try to control the controlling. You're fucked if you like it or not. No one remains virgin, sooner or later life fucks everyone and not the way one likes it. There is a song by Johnny Cash – God will cut you down and that's the tiger's mouth. That's the pointer.

Whatever you believe in, will drop dead in one second and no one ever cared about it and nothing will happen. By all your questions, techniques of control of trying to avoid discomfort – Bing!! – whatever has a face, is ugly. There are only ugly faces. Every morning you look in the mirror and say 'Oh my dear ugly face'. You only see the wrinkles and you try everything against aging and you know you will lose.

[Pointing to another visitor]: You've shaved today...

Q: I'm trying to harmonize...

K: You try to harmonize by looking nice but it works only for a moment. Then comes the inner unshaved one. [Laughter] The inner ass-hole pops up again and that you cannot shave. [Laughter] The ugly beast, you want to hide all the time. The inner beast and you want to tame that inner beast. But everyone is beasty because whatever has to 'be' – is beasty, angry. Then you make the futile attempt to tame that beast. In the circus of life, there are many directors who want to tame it – the bull fighters. The *sufis* have different techniques..

Q [Another visitor]: They pray...

K: A nice prayer is 'I don't care', many use it. It's like a *mantra*. You try to disconnect from whatever happened by saying 'But I don't care'. But as much as you don't want to worry, you worry about it. Crazy! No way out! The more you want to disconnect, you are connected. You make it real. Fantastic! Even if your wife dies in a car accident, you come out of the car and say 'No worries mate'. It's an Australian *mantra*. There's a song in America – 'We shall overcome'. What came over me? [Laughter]

You always expect something worse. That's your inner *mantra*. You expect something really bad because if it's not so bad, it's already good. It's a vagabond technique, but it doesn't work. Nothing works! Even being everywhere just for one day, shit is there, because 'you' are there. Even if you are not connected to that place and can easily let-go, that one who easily lets go – is shit. No way out! But they try.

That's the Buddhist technique, they show you your failure. You cannot fail because wherever you are, 'you' are and wherever 'you' are, it's shit. That's Buddhism. Buddhism is a religion of failures, always pointing to the failure. Christianity is the opposite, they say you're absolutely guilty – maximum *culpa*. In Buddhism they reduce you to the minimum and in Christianity they want to put you to the maximum. In both ways, they want to get rid of 'you', but it doesn't work!

Religions never worked, thank God! But they try and they try very hard. Then they have mystics in the religion. Like the *sufis* and the Christian mystics.

Okay my dear failures – have a nice failing day. [Laughter] Be happy that you don't have to be happy.

February 21, 2012. Morning Talk.
Thailand

Even the understanding – 'Everything is consciousness' – is bullshit

Q: I was thinking about Radha Ma and the only thing I was wondering was about the advantage that came about by writing the letter...

K: It's like a romance, being totally disappointed with the beloved. She blamed the dearest disciples, they all turned away from her. She blamed them for putting her into the situation of total disappointment. It was a broken heart story. They did not do what she wanted them to do. For many years she tried to do best for them, spiritually. And then they turned away from her and then there was a broken heart. It was like a love story from both sides. Do you think the guru does not have the investment in so-called disciples? Imagine I would expect something from the people here!

Q: I thought she was getting away from them...

K: No. She always tried to get them back. It was just like between two lovers – broken heart story. It's all about this bloody romance bullshit. Of course, there's a love affair going on – everywhere. Not in that sense, but in a higher sense.

Q [Another visitor]: I have a love affair here [pointing to herself]...

K: With your shit you have a love affair, I know. And then you're totally pissed – that this piece of shit does not do what you want. You would even kill yourself if this piece of shit would not work anymore. You love your finger more than yourself. It's all like Romeo and Juliet. You would kill yourself if your beloved does not function for you.

Q: Because it makes you feel special...

K: Not special. You just don't feel lonely anymore. That you found something that fits you. And then there is harmony. Now you're in harmony with a little piece of shit and you don't want to miss it.

What does this God try to do in this consciousness? Try to find someone or something he can be in harmony with, what he can love, what he doesn't want to change anymore. That's called love, you find something that is okay. And then you want to stick to that. Then when it's not okay, you get pissed and then you want a revenge and want to kill it. Because it's not living up to your expectations. Then you want to go away from your beloved, you want a divorce.

It's like that in every relationship. The moment you found the perfect fit, you fall in love with that image you expected. And when it doesn't live up to that expectation, you kick it out. You're pissed and you're really disappointed. Then you're whining – poor me, it didn't work again, I was hoping this time it would be different.

And that is the same with this bloody body. You meditate so much and do yoga and make your body perfect to your expectations – and then you have a back pain. You're let down by shit, by an expectation. It's crazy! In the whole universe, God is looking for it's beloved – for it's true love.

Q [Another visitor]: This is a story of harm and harmony...

K: Yeah. You want to be harmed – never. You want the harm, the misery to end. And you think that there is something that will end the misery. For the same reason you fall in love with your guru. You think there is someone who can end the misery. And for that, you go to him. You expect him to end your misery.

Q: And when it doesn't work you want to harm him or yourself...

K: Then you want to kill him.

Q [Another visitor]: So, it's a dangerous business that you're in...

K: Yeah. [Laughter] I hate you all from the beginning, I have no problem. I don't expect anything from you.

Q [Another visitor]: Hating wouldn't help, it's the same...

K: *Neti-neti* is always fine – neither-neither. There will be never anyone who will be worth listening to what I say. I think in Radha's case there was still an expectation that she can help somebody with energy. And there is something going on with energy, but it's always disappointing. There's always like a child God who wants to find his mother where he can go back and find home with someone and rest forever in the presence.

And you cannot stop it. It will be like this forever. It's like this in every relationship, every romance, every friendship in the school. You thought you found your perfect mate. This is made for me, only for me, your soul mate. All those satsangs in America, people are going for soul mates. Not for truth.

Q [Another visitor]: It it chemical?

K: It's just your genetic design from ancestors giving you an image of a perfect mate – what fits you, visual, emotional and chemical. And that's called falling in love with an image, what fits to this image. There's a resonance. In that resonance there's a – Yes! You don't know why but there's a 'Yes' coming from all of that. And sooner or later for sure comes – 'Maybe'. And out of a 'maybe' you become pissed and then you only see the bad things. And then it's totally 'No' – No, no, no. But then you're already clinged-on and it's really hard to cling-off. And then it hurts.

It's all meant to be like this. The totality fits in that moment and then it's called love and then it's a misfit again. It cannot fit forever.

Q [Another visitor]: So, this happens to partners, children, *gurus*?

K: It's the same fitting, the same story.

Q [Another visitor]: Is there anything wrong about that?

K: No. I just show that it's temporary. It cannot be forever.

Q: So, is it okay that way?

K: It's okay but it's not okay. Because you're looking for something eternal. You're looking for an eternal home, not a temporary one. You're always looking for that harmony, that peace which will be there forever. For this temporary one, you know that you will be disappointed anyway. If you see it will end anyway – okay, why not? But your heart always goes for eternity – for truth. And then you will be disappointed. Then it hurts. You will suffer again. If that's not a problem, then there's no problem.

Q [Another visitor]: But the suffering happens also if you stay on your own…

K: That's why the hermits go to the Himalayas to exercise being alone. And they can do it for a while. But then they take the world with them. You cannot be alone.

Q: No. That's what I mean…

K: The misery will not end. There's a temporary pause in misery, but then the misery starts again. The sadness of being alone, you cannot escape. No way! But what to do? You try everything and nothing works. Even Buddha tried everything to avoid disharmony and he failed. He called himself as the biggest failure ever and so what? From there comes – what to do? You try everything and then – what to do?

Then you try again – but without 'trying'. It's a play, you just play. It's all a play anyway. But if you take it seriously, you're in trouble. It's a serious shit, but shit happens! Not to do it is as bad as doing it. So, what?

This dance of consciousness, trying to find a perfect match with itself will never stop. This inquiry is an infinite game. It will always dance with itself and look for a perfect dancer, a perfect dance, a perfect harmony. And temporarily maybe there's – Yes! This is it! The illusion is there. And then there is the disillusion.

That's why when Yudhistira was in hell, Krishna asked him – Are you ready to be in hell forever? Is there any tendency left to avoid this hell? Because that's the 'me' – this little tendency to avoid hell. This game of trying. And he said – No! There is no tendency of avoidance. And then there is not even a hell anymore. And then there is what? You don't even know what it is. And then there is no one who's alone – never was. There's just what-you-are and that can never be alone because there is no 'one' who could be alone.

But the tendency of avoidance is for the one who's alone. And he always tries to be not alone. But you have to be with this tendency. You cannot stop it. It came by itself and it will be gone by itself. But not by your doing something against it. The wish for knowing yourself, you cannot wish away. Because the wish of wishing the wish away is even worse than the wish of wishing.

John Klien was very artistic in describing this. He said the wishlessness of your nature is like a wishlessness of joy. Out of that comes a wish – to know oneself. And the wish came by itself and it will be gone by itself. It's an appearance and a disappearance – that's all. If you want to make it disappear earlier, you're in trouble. Just see that it came and it will be gone – sooner or later. But who cares when?

It's like this body – it came to you and it will be gone one day. And you will be again what you were before this body was there. And your nature doesn't have any persona or mask. And there's no lover. Because you're with and without that lover. Every night you go to that – you are That, without the body tendencies.

Back to Radha, this is still the Romeo and Juliet story. It doesn't stop with *gurus*. What to do? You will be fucked anyway. Have a coffee. [sipping coffee] The next sip of coffee is good enough.

Any questions for 2012? Everyone hopes for the final year!

Q [Another visitor]: Hopes for what?

K: 22nd December this year, there should be a transformation of human consciousness into the next level. Since Eckhart Tolle and new earth talk about it, everyone hopes for it. [Laughter]

Q: And what happens when nothing happens?

K: The same as every year. There will be New Year [Laughter] and then the next hope. In 1999 there was the millennium hope and in 1993 there were light workers making the light circles. How many times do we have to repeat that? The end of the Mayan calendar is just because the stone was ending there. [Laughter]

In America everyone talks about it and there's even a movie. I say if that consciousness which can be transmuted or transformed into a higher level, what kind of bullshit consciousness would that be? – A relative one. And who gives a fuck about a relative consciousness? You and Me.

Q [Another visitor]: Even the *sufis* are ready to fight…

K: You see, even the *sufis* are in that! There's a Rumi – a rumour in the sufi world.

Q [Another visitor]: Now you're suddenly talking about a bullshit consciousness…

K: Yeah. I talk about the human consciousness. Who gives a fuck about human consciousness?

Q: Who are the humans?

K: I tell you – Eckhart Tolle is a human.

Q: Really?

K: He says so!

Q: Why don't you see him as consciousness?

K: For me it's no problem but he sees himself as human consciousness that needs to be transformed to a higher level.

Q: No. You're the one having a problem right now...

K: With what?

Q: With him...

K: I always have a problem with him because he bullshits everybody.

Q: How can he do that when there's only consciousness?

K: Consciousness is bullshitting all the time.

Q: So what? Why do you care?

K: Why shouldn't I care? [Laughter] Now you're better than everybody else? [Laughter] Now you're the special consciousness who doesn't care anymore. Now you have a problem, that someone else has a problem. You cannot get out of it, but you try very hard. There will always be people announcing that something will happen at sometime. And the hope would rise again.

Q [Another visitor]: Wouldn't it be nice if everybody would be enlightened in one step?

K: No!

Q: Why not?

K: Then there would be someone who could be enlightened – that would be hell already. That's the idea of hell. That there is one who needs to be enlightened. And that's already too much. That there is a possibility of enlightenment – it's hell. Because that there is a possibility of hell, means that there's one who needs to be enlightened. That's the biggest trap ever! Then working on that enlightenment is what we're living in. Trying to become what-you-are. Then you suffer about it.

Any moment you try to become what-you-are, you're not what-you-are. Because you imagine that you have to become what-you-are. So, there's a misery of you trying to become what you already are. And saying that there's a possibility of enlightenment, that there would be a moment, is feeding that story. Okay, why not? It will continue forever.

But just pointing it out that there's nothing in here, is as same shit as everything. It's like Obama promising harmony in America. It's like Eckhart Tolle promising the transmutation of consciousness. There's no difference of promises. And the whole universe is living by promises. Every wife promises the husband that I'll make you happy and the husband promises the same – from the beginning. Every mother has a child because she thinks that the baby will make her happy. It's always promises. So, what to do? You cannot stop it.

But I'm here to point it out. Otherwise I should go home and be quiet and watch television. Then I should say – Everything is consciousness, no problem. I should say it once and then I go home. [Laughter] If that pleases someone, he should go home and watch television. But this is fun. Destroying all these teachers and *gurus* is fun. Everyone has to be destroyed for you to be what-you-are – even yourself. Even the idea of Self has to be destroyed in that sense. And I try my best, but I know it doesn't work. But still I try.

Q [Another visitor]: Destroyer is a good name for you...

K: [Laughing] What is *Shiva*? He destroys the idea of *Shiva* when it comes to that point. The whole universe has to be chopped.

Q [Another visitor]: My suffering phantom wants to be enlightened in a permanent way...

K: You want to be happy forever.

Q: And when you say that existence doesn't care, doesn't know you...

K: It knows you absolutely, but not as your problems.

Q: Sometimes I reach a point of very strong despair. At night sometimes I dream of you and other masters and there's a sense of embracing and I feel energy and I can start again...

K: And you get extra energy for daily life.

Q: Somewhere I see that I'm creating it...

K: Your nature which is consciousness creates circumstance and pampers you with some energy with some faces and names. But it's all you – building yourself up again for the daily life. But it's not an outside guru thing or something.

Q: The effect is real...

K: Yeah. Your whole body gets energized.

Q: What is that?

K: You go astray in the world and you feel fucked-up again and then you get weak and weak. And then you go into a wellness treatment for yourself. Then you give it names and forms and you get centered again in that energy. And all your body cells get alive again. And you go on again. It's like a technique of rejuvenation.

Q: It's like being in love again and fooling myself?

K: No. You just go astray and then you get centered again into That what is the energy.

Q: But being centered is astray as well?

K: No. You stay in That what is peace and energy. And then you're stupid enough to go out again and get tired. In India, they say – stay in the shade. When you know the shade, stay in the shade. Then you don't go astray with your senses.

Q: If I could stay in the shade, I would stay in the shade...

K: Every moment you want to stay in the shade, you cannot. Because then you think there's one who needs to stay in the shade.

Q: Then why do you say – stay in the shade?

K: Because, if you could stay in the shade, that would be the best. But you cannot!

Q: Exactly…

K: But it would happen again. You go out and then you go back to the shade again. You will be refreshed again and then you go out and get fucked again.

Q: It's tiring…

K: So what? As I said in the beginning, you cannot stay there. You have to go out again. You have to be what-you-are in being fucked and not being fucked being what-you-are. If you can be what-you-are in being not fucked, you're depending on being not fucked. You have to be in both senses. And you are in both senses – what-you-are. And you cannot stay anywhere.

The Taoists, they try to be in the *samadhi* of shade. You're just fine in that awareness pool, choicelessness, they stay in there for thousands of years. But then they have to come out, sooner or later and they have go to the market place. And they are as thirsty as before. So, it doesn't stop. It doesn't matter how long you stay there, sooner or later you will end up in this place again and you will be fucked again.

There's a scene. One master goes to a market and wants to drink but falls into *samadhi*. Then he wakes up from that timelessness and the next moment he has to drink and get drunk. So, there is no time for a while. Then you start again in the same instant you left. You have to continue the bloody story. The story waits for you.

Q: When you come back in the story…

K: There's no back. You don't come back. The perception just disconnects.

Q: The perception is connected with the story?

K: It doesn't get connected. It's never connected. It shifts between different ways of experiencing yourself. And this is a fucking hell experience. So what? You can only fuck in hell.

Q: The veil of separation...

K: There is no veil. For the perception, there is no veil. In what? For who?

Q: But the 'me' comes back...

K: But the 'me' was still there. It cannot come back, it was always there. There is no come back. It waits for you – Hello! Here I am! Ha Ha. Then Kiya shifts from there – where there is no Kiya – fine. Then there is Kiya – [making a growling sound]. No Kiya – Fine. Kiya – Aww [making a howling sound].

And still perception has no problem.

Q: So, what is this dropping?

K: What dropping? No 'dropping'.

Q: So, what happened for you?

K: Nothing happened. Every morning Karl waits for me.

Q: But it's not sticky...

K: I'm absolutely stuck to what-I-Am. And you don't want to be stuck, that makes you discomfortable.

Q: Of course...

K: You don't want to be what-you-are and that makes you suffer. You are That. You don't want to be Kiya. So, you don't want to have one aspect of your nature. You want to avoid.

Q: I want to be Kiya and the dark one, but without that belief...

K: That is Kiya. The one who wants only the good things and not the bad things. That's the name of 'me'. Kiya wants only comfort.

Q: I'm okay to care and suffer, but without this caring of it...

K: You see, you want to change something.

Q: Of course!

K: So what? [Laughter]

Q: I wouldn't sit here otherwise...

K: And that makes you sit in hell.

Q: Yeah. For me, sitting here is the best hell that can happen...

K: Only if I could say that. [Laughter]

Q: But you don't seem to care, that's the whole point...

K: I care.

Q: But you don't care that you care and I still care that I care... [Laughter]

K: You know I care, I always wash clothes.

Q: I want your advantage...

K: My advantage? You want to have my absolute disadvantage.

Q: Exactly! The absolute advantage and the absolute disadvantage. And I'm going to sit here...

Q [Another visitor]: We want to have your relative advantage...

K: Which one? [Laughter]

Q: The advantage that you don't care that you care. That's the relative advantage...

K: That's good enough for me. For me, to be what-you-cannot-not-be means you are That. And there is no way out. And this is an absolute disadvantage. But who cares?

Q: But in manifest, it's a relative advantage...

K: No. I still have to shit and I still have to drink. I have to talk to you. Come on!

Q: You go through whatever you have to go through. But you don't care. This is the relative advantage...

K: You make something out of it. I give a shit.

Q: All of us here are for relative advantage...

K: Of course. Wellness club! I know people come for that and they pay. If they get ease by that, why not? Sooner or later the hell waits for them anyway. [Laughter] Then they listen again. It's like being in a shade. Listening to it puts you in a shade, like a pill. But then you have to go out again – sooner or later.

But why not? For me, it's just to see the difference that you cannot stay there forever. That you can stay there for a long time by little help, by listening. I know that calms you down. But you cannot stay there. You always come back to the trouble. It can be calmed down. But what can be calmed down will start again – in whatever way.

And maybe in one split second, you see that it will never end. And there's an absolute insight – so what? I'm here what I Am and I'm there what I Am. May it be this way or that way. May it be as it is. If it's like this, it's like this. If it's like that, it's like that. Who cares? This who cares is just like the split second. Why not? Whatever happens then – okay or not.

But it's all about showing you that this is temporary and that is temporary. And you will always shift between all those possibilities. But what-you-are has nothing to lose or gain in it. That peace – which is what-you-are – was never lost in the trouble and cannot be gained in no-trouble and cannot be reached in what is the beyond. From the beyond, you end up there and there and you will always come back to – this. It's like in *Yogavashishta* – see you next time.

All the realizations, all those precious things you can achieve, will be gone – sooner or later and you will end up in this one. This is one way of you realizing yourself and you are That what is realizing itself – whether you like it or not. There will never be any end to it. It's just one way. But this way is just absolute one way – as the other ones are. So, I try to talk to myself and not bullshit myself by telling that there is a place you can land.

No! There is no place you can land forever. Temporarily you

can land there – but only temporarily. Even the understanding 'Everything is consciousness' is bullshit! It's a temporary understanding and you will drop out again. Kill the idea that you can kill something – by being what-you-are. Because what-you-are can never be killed.

Q [Another visitor]: Sometimes I plug my ear phones and I forget to switch-on. And I listen and listen…

K: It's not going on, but you listen to the talk. It's in your head already. [Laughter]

Q: And then I think, maybe one day I don't need it…

K: Maybe. Then you always have Karl in your background. You don't have to plug-in anymore. [Laughter] Plugged in, forever!

Q [Another visitor]: Everything I say or think or do, is looking for a conclusion…

K: You want to finish yourself. You want to reach the end and you don't care what happens then, but you want to end it. All whatever happens, is to end it. It's like a permanent suicide attempt of consciousness wanting to end it. Whatever it does, all the romances, all the enlightenment, all the meditation, is trying to end it. But it cannot be ended. This never ending story continues – if you like it or not and no one ever did it. Whoever claimed that he made it – forget it!

Q: And therefore the end of tendency of avoidance is not a happening…

K: It's already there because what-you-are never had any tendencies. And just by being what-you-are, there's no tendency at all. But the imaginary phantom you wake up with, will always have a tendency. And you cannot stop it. There will always be one kind of tendency that this body has. There is an infinite story of tendencies of consciousness.

And the main tendency is, consciousness wanting to know

consciousness. The lover wants to know the beloved – wants to know himself. That's the main tendency. And that's the way you realize yourself. You cannot otherwise realize yourself. This lie that the lover is different from the beloved, is already there when you wake up. That experience of awareness, is already an experience of separation. So, there's a false evidence – as an experience. And you want to end that.

Out of love for yourself, you want to end separation – naturally. And that will never stop, because you end what is not there. There is a false evidence of separation and that false evidence, you take as real. And that makes you longing for the end of it. And the longing will not end, because the moment you are separated, even in that fake imaginary experience, you long to end it – out of love.

How can you not wake up and by waking up no one wakes up? It's too late when you're there. And when you wake up, you are already out of what-you-are – in an experience. But it's only an experience. You never went out. That's the trick. It seems like you went out – to whatever experience. But by experiencing of being out, the experience does not make you different from what-you-are. You never went out! You never left what-you-are.

But now, your imagination became real. And now you want to go back. But as more you want to go back, you confirm a fake. That's the whole consciousness. God started to know himself. And by knowing himself, there are two Gods. He creates his own hell. He became a lover, falling in love with his beloved – with himself. And now he wants to control his beloved by knowing his beloved – all the best and the bad. But wanting to have the best, is sometimes not so good.

Any wanting, any tendency is bad. Even a good tendency, is a bad tendency. In that sense, having a tendency is always bad. Being what-you-are, has no tendency. But being what-you-are-not, already has tendency of something you feel, it cannot be that. Then you try something. But you cannot stop it. The love affair with yourself will not end. So, you try your best, but it's never good enough. Because by whatever you try or do or understand, you cannot become what-you-are – Impossible!

Nisargadatta said, 'Who Am I?' is the best you can do. But by whatever you do, you cannot attain what-you-are. Never! Nothing is good enough. But still you have to do it. And the best you can do is – Who Am I? – being concentrated on what-you-are. And staying in That – if you can – because already that's like being in the shade of awareness. Because there the story burns out. That's the best you can do, but it's not good enough.

So, yes, you can do something. But whatever you do, even the best you can do, is not good enough. Because none of that will make you what-you-are. And by only being what-you-are, what-you-cannot-not-be, is peace itself. Not knowing any peace and not needing any peace.

But everything else, any peace which comes by techniques, is good. But not good enough.

Q: Because there is still a second?

K: It's part of realization. But you cannot find reality in realization. And the realization has seven different ways, but none of them is what-you-are. There are differences of realizing yourself. But none of those differences, can lead to what-you-are. You are already That, what is reality realizing itself. But not one way of realizing those realizations make you what you already are. Never!

And you have to be in this worst case scenario here. This hell of separation experiences, of being a human. It's really the worse of the worse. Having emotions, having all the bullshit running is the worst case scenario you can be in. If you cannot be in this scenario what-you-are, you will not become it in any other one. And this will always wait for you. This Romeo and Juliet bullshit.

Q [Another visitor]: Very good talking *guruji*, you never mentioned the word shit even one time. [Laughter] You're pointing to the absolute but you've never mentioned this horrible word. You're talking like a man from Oxford... [Laughter]

K: I'm an ox now – para-ox. No bullshit anymore when you are an ox – then you become an para-ox.

I can only sit here and point out – No way out! You can come here with experiences and you can come with techniques and we can talk about it. And maybe I can show you just another way of experiencing yourself. But even that is as empty as all the other ways.

Q [Another visitor]: But with experiences and changes, can't life improve a lot? For example, I was a heavy smoker and I quit. That's one hell I left. I was an alcoholic, that's another hell I left. I improved my health. So, today I have a life which I feel much better than twenty years before. These changes and improvements...

K: Then it will end and the worms will have a feast.

Q: But right now, it improves a lot...

K: And I have nothing against it. But this is a relative life that can be improved and will be gone one day. I have nothing against it – why not?

But as alcohol gave you up, alcohol can take you again. As smoking gave you up, smoking can take you again. As sickness gave you up, sickness can take you again. You're not safe, my dear.

Q: That's what I don't believe...

K: Now you think you're in control. But this control can be taken away because it was given to you – if you like it or not – any moment is dangerous. The circumstance can be so extreme and so different, that it can make a difference – you know that. As you knew before, the alcohol came to you and it can come again – you know that.

If your destiny now is that you're sober and maybe your destiny is supposed to change next week to the opposite, then it will change, if you like it or not. No one is in any control, I tell you. As you cannot decide which mother to have or if you're born or not, you cannot decide whether you drink the next drink, or not.

Q: We have opposite opinions. I don't agree...

K: I know because you have to be like this because you imagined that you made it. That by your will power, you made it. But this will power was given to you and can be taken away – any moment. By whatever circumstance, I don't want to make a big picture. But if totality wants it, it will happen, as it happened before.

I don't want it to happen. I don't want anything to change. But I'm just saying, your will power was given and it can be taken – anyway. So, it's your will power. But I like it that it's not in your hand. You're not the doer of your destiny, you're not deciding it – not at all!

Q: I cannot get the will power through the meditations that I'm practicing?

K: No! It comes when it comes. It's there when it's there, but not because you want it. Even God cannot want what he wants! If he could want what he wants do you imagine that this world would be as it is?

If the goodness itself – God as the goodness itself, in nature, could that goodness itself, make all the happenings that you see around? If God could want what he wants, out of his goodness, out of his love, being love itself, how can it be like it is, if he could decide how it has to be? Big question.

And I tell you, even God cannot want what he wants. He has to dream the dream as the dream has to be dreamt and not otherwise. And as you have to be played by the consciousness, you're being played this way. And it can change at any moment. It's all unpredictable and that I like. No one has any control about anything, and there's no one who can decide what he does. So, there's no sin, there's no guilt in anything.

If you now would be guilty for your good behavior, you would be guilty for your bad behavior. Maybe the circumstance happens that you do something really bad. Then you would be in the same belief system – You did it. Now it's like heaven and then it would be like hell because it would put the entire burden on you.

Q: That's the reason I don't do it...

K: Only because you want to have a good conscience. That's the only good reason otherwise if you kill everybody, then you're not a good person. Only because you want to sleep well, you don't kill people because you want to sleep well. That sounds good. [Laughter]

Q [Another visitor]: In any addiction there is always first a surrender, then there is control again...

K: But what can they do? It's opening and closing. It's always like that, but first you have to admit that I'm powerless.

Q [Another visitor]: Yeah...

K: But you say, I have power – I did it. How can you say I'm powerless and still do it?

Q: I can decide for today...

K: You cannot decide for today. When you say, I'm powerless, the decision is made by the moment, not by you. Otherwise you'd have power to decide. You have no power to decide. If you really would admit I'm powerless – fine. Because you have no power.

Q: But you get power...

K: The power will happen. The power for you to say 'no again' to the next, will be there or not. The acceptance that you're powerless has to be there. And then the decision will be made. It's not your decision, otherwise you're in trouble again.

[Joking] I like junkies actually... [Laughter]

Q [Another visitor]: Could we say to our physician that I am just the spirit and I don't have any hands or legs or body but still I Am...

K: Yeah. Without legs you can re-legs. [Laughter] Then you don't have to go anymore, so you can relax.

Q: But I don't have any hands...

K: If you don't have any hands, nothing is in your hand.

Q: I have no brain so I cannot figure out anything...

K: If you have no brain, you have no thinking. That's what I'm talking about, what-you-are has no ownership. There is no owning anything. This ownership idea is God owning existence. Even by existing he owns existence and with that the bloody ownership starts.

Q [Another visitor]: If I look at your website, you have an agenda planned till the end of the year. Who decides that? Is it you or is it the power?

K: People ask me to come and sometimes it's yes and sometimes it's a no. I don't know. I like to have an agenda so that I know where I have to be at that time. So, I'm free of thinking because I don't have to imagine what else can I do, as I have to sit there anyway. Like here, three weeks, twice a day, I have nothing to worry about. I have to sit here anyway. [Laughter] It comes as it comes. It's like an ant running over my feet, I cannot decide. I can just pick it up and kill it. It's the same with schedules, I wonder how it happens – moment-by-moment. It's always like a reaction. It's like when you have an itch, you scratch it without thinking that you have to scratch yourself.

Q: So, you don't plan, you react?

K: Sometimes planning happens – yes. And then decisions are made, but I don't take them so personal. [Laughter] Some have the trick to take the success personal and disaster as impersonal. [Laughter] Actually, I take everything absolute personal – I Am That and whatever happens, is what-I-Am and I've done everything. I'm absolutely guilty for all the bullshit that happens – And I don't care, because I'm absolutely guilty for what-is and what-is-not. Because this is what I Am.

This is more than easy because if you're guilty for little things, you really have a bad conscience or a good conscience, but if you're the consciousness itself that has done everything, the absolute doership or non-doership, nothing is done by doing. Because if you're absolutely guilty for whatever is and is-not – who cares? If you're guilty for the smallest and the biggest bullshit in this bloody universe, who cares? If you're guilty for a part of it then you care. And then you compare with others – what is your guilt? And what is my guilt?

No! This is all what you are. And you're guilty for all the bullshit and all the junkies and all the non-junkies and all the addicts and the non-addicts and you're guilty for all that murdering and raping – whatever-is. What to do? And nothing happens.

Q [Another visitor]: But then you don't have that sense of guilt anymore...

K: Absolute guilt! I'm absolutely guilty!

Q: But it's not a painful guilt for you...

K: No? I pay everything. I pay myself. It's very painful. [Laughter]

Q: It seems that you enjoy your guilt...

K: I don't have to enjoy the guilt. There's just no way out. There's peace because there's no way out of guilt. When you can clean up your guilt, then you are in pain.

Q: But at that moment, it's not an entertainment but it sounds like one...

K: It's a split second. It's not a second – it's splitting the second. How often do I have to say that it's not a moment? Why do you repeat that it's a moment? It's splitting the second.

Q: But you're sure...

K: It's not sure, there is no second. It's splitting the second – by being what-you-are, there is no idea of second. There is no lover, no beloved – You are That. It's not a moment. Every night you do it.

Q: From my side...

K: There is no – your side.

Q: When there's deep-deep sleep, there is a moment when it drops...

K: But dropping is in time and I'm not talking about time. I'm talking about just being what-you-are and there is no second. That's splitting the idea of second – just by being what-you-are. And it's not in a second.

Q: I understand that...

K: You don't understand that. You still call it a moment.

Q: For me it still sounds like a happening...

K: You want to see it as a happening because otherwise you would collapse. It's your little hope. I'm not your little fucking hope. [Laughter]

Q: Oh yes you are... [Laughter]

Q [Another visitor]: This is what happens in church, by your confessions. You go in there and say all your bad things...

K: That I would say too. The maximum guilt leads you to absolution. *Mea culpa* – maximum *culpa*. You're maximum *culpa*. And in That, there's a relaxation, there's an absolution in it. What to do? May it be as it is. That's the maximum *culpa*. What to do? So, in that sense, in church there's something that's not so bad. It's a good pointer sometimes, so you can't say everything is bad, just because there's a German pope. [Laughter]

Q [Another visitor]: Splitting the second, is splitting the other...

K: Yeah. In splitting the second, it's just being what-you-are, being what-is. That's splitting the second. There's no me and no you. That's splitting the second. It's not in a split second.

Q: Splitting the sense of separation...

K: The book of Papaji about split second is not about moment in time where you have an insight. No! Splitting the second happens every night, by being what-you-are. And by being what-you-are, there's no second – you are That! And That is maximum *culpa*. You're the absolute owner of what-is – you are That! You are That what is realization. But you're not the one who's realizing itself.

But you are sitting here to get minimized to be maximized. [Laughter]

Q: Yeah. That's the idea...

K: Yeah. When you're nothing, you're everything – that's the paradox. When you're the emptiness, you're the fullness. It's always That when you go to the minimum you're the maximum. But if you're in middle – you're in shit. [Laughter] That's the middle finger. [Laughter]

Q [Another visitor]: If I want to take a decision in a conscious moment, I go into meditation or I run for a hundred kilometers...

K: But that's meditation too because you reach a dead point and then no one is running.

Q: And then sometimes I come to a state, where I know. There's an answer to the question and it's absolutely clear. Where does this come from?

K: Because the knower drops. That's why they call it the dead point, where the 'me' drops and there's natural knowledge, natural understanding.

Q: When I follow this, I'm always right. When I start discussion about it and decide something different...

K: Then you're in right and wrong and then even the right is wrong. But over there, there is no right and wrong. It's like an absolute yes – the vertical.

Q: What happens to me is that when it happens, sometimes strange things appear. And then after that, my mind begins to discuss if this is right or wrong...

K: Yeah. The devil wakes up again.

Q: So, follow it...

K: If you can. If not, you cannot. But I know it's the vertical spirit that knows as knowing. And then comes the discussion. But you never know who wins. The vertical knows – and then the devil starts again, discussing. It's disgusting! And sometimes you reach that point and sometimes not. And you cannot stay there because you always fall back to the discussion. So, what to do?

No, I have no technique. If you could, you would stay in the knowing. But any moment you want to stay there, you're out of it. You reach it by whatever and the next moment you're out. I have no advise for that.

Q: No way to put the devils away?

K: No.

Q: Shit! [Laughter]

K: I would say, little bit of mind-fuck is not so bad. Let there be sex – let the mind-fuck itself. The body will always have the tendencies of fighting and doing things. It's part of the system – tendencies fighting against tendencies. It's phantoms fighting against phantoms, shadows fighting shadows. What to do?

And that what is the vertical – the spirit, is anyway there. But you always end up in the fighting again. When Nisargadatta was dying in the last moments he said, 'Now with this body, all the tendencies of this body are leaving me. Whatever happened to this body before are leaving now with this body and there's still no one who cares'.

So, that carelessness of its nature is permanent. The caring and the not-caring, the knowing and the not-knowing belongs to this body. Even the vertical knowing belongs to the body. It comes with this body and will leave with this body, but the carelessness is the screen where the caring and not-caring, the knowing and the not-knowing, the discussion, the fucking and the not-fucking happens. It's un-spoiled, there's no spot on it. It's as it was before – spotless.

All the movements of this body, all the tendencies, they happened and will happen until the last breath of this so-called 'entity'. And at that instant, all go with that and there's still no one who cares, as now, there's no one who cares. There's carelessness of what is your nature that you call perception – un-spoiled. It was there before and it will be after that – movie and story of this body – there is what-you-are – un-spoiled that doesn't even know anything. There's neither knowing or not knowing. There's neither vertical or horizontal. It's always that where the horizontal and the vertical happens. And nothing happened.

By all that happenings of you experiencing yourself as a junkie, an addict, an alcoholic, a smoker, all of that will be gone in one instant. As it came, it will be gone. All the actions and all the decisions and all the tendencies, which came with the body will be gone [blowing in the wind] as it was never there before.

And all that what happens, running marathon of hundred kilometers or two hundred kilometers, all that story in one instant will – Ping! – as if nothing ever happened. And being now that screen, nothing ever happened which you cannot-not-be anyway. It's just so easy and so natural, all the rest – being involved – you cannot stop. This movie will continue until the last frame. Then something else happens. This screen didn't came with the body and will not go with the body. The screen will just start another movie. Whatever it will be, the next frame will be there – without the body, but something else will happen. There will be no end of it.

As that screen which is there [pointing to the visitor] in which the movie of the body happens, is the same screen in which movie of this body [pointing to himself] happens. Because there is no two. There's only one perception – the eye of God. And that is experiencing this [pointing to himself] as that [pointing to the visitor]. In nature, there's no difference. That what is experiencing this body, is experiencing that body. The screen in which this body story happens is the same screen where that body story happens. The whole universe happens on That screen – on the eye of God.

And being this eye of God – you cannot not be. That's the effortlessness of being what-you-are. And everything else, all the efforts happen by themselves. All the movements, all the movie is already happening by itself. And you cannot have any influence. You are the almighty – the reality itself. But you cannot change your own movie. Because it's already done. All the babies are already born and whatever is born is already dead.

If you read the Mahabharata, Arjuna wants to become a pacifist but he has to go to the war and kill all the enemies and all the friends. What Krishna says is, 'They're already dead, you cannot kill someone who's already dead. So, you have to do your duty, if you like it or not'. So, if you have to do it anyway – What to do?

You cannot kill anybody. There's only shadows you can kill. As there's no killer here, there's no one to kill there.

Q [Another visitor]: But there's never a blank screen?

K: Every night you have a blank screen and every morning, Christa waits for you and Kiya waits for the split-moment on the screen.

Q [Another visitor]: Is the totality analogous to the root 'I'?

K: The root 'I' is the screen, then there is the first notion of awareness starts in it – that you fall in love with it. You fall in love with your first image – the first awareness. And you cannot stop it. That what-you-are becomes I-I – the eye of the eye – the realizer. And then the realizer is realizing itself as a lover realizing itself in a beloved. This story you cannot stop. You cannot not identify yourself with the 'I'. You are the nature of the 'I'. So, being the 'I' – it's too late. That's why I say, it's too late.

Q: When we have this discussion then something happens and I find myself in it... [Laughter]

K: That's part of the story. One wakes up – in what? That's called waking up from the horizontal action to the vertical. Then one is awake – different story – but still a story. So, there's a horizontal separation and then there is a vertical oneness story. But both is story because where there is horizontal, there is vertical. So, where there is separation and oneness, there is horizontal and vertical oneness.

No-time and time – both come together. And it's permanently there, right now there's time, no-time and even the screen – awareness – all of that is there. But you cannot decide in what way you experience yourself. The moment you want to be vertical, you're horizontal – for sure. [Laughter] When you're the vertical, there's no problem. But the moment you want to stay in it, you're the horizontal. Because it's so nice in the vertical, you want to stay there. But by trying to stay there, you're in the horizontal. It's *kaput* [German for broken].

How many stories do we have from Papaji with oneness experience given by the master? For two months, three months, staying in that vertical – whatever. And then dropping out again. They lost it again – they lost the pearl. They didn't polish it enough. And then they feel so guilty that they have not worked enough on it. There master gave them the precious thing and then they lost it again, they feel so guilty. [Jokingly whining] Oh, it was given and I lost it again.

For sure, what can be given, can be lost again. And what you can reach, you have to leave again. So, look at what can be given and who can give you something? You find that only the devil can give you something. That you call Lucifer – the guru who promises you enlightenment and something better. But what to do?

And then they create a *satguru*, who makes you sat. But that *satguru* has no lineage. He destroys all the lineages and all the relationships.

Q [Another visitor]: In *Yogavashishta*, Rama asked, 'Nothing is in your hands, so how can you live in this world?' and Vashishta replied that, 'You have to know that but you still have to continue doing what you need to do'...

K: That's what Mohammad said to everyone – Inshallah, but bind your camel.

Q: So, if you think nothing is in your hand but still it's not possible to not do things...

K: No. You cannot do that. No one can sit somewhere and not do anything.

Q [Another visitor]: But binding your camel or not binding your camel is not in your hands...

K: What he meant by the question is that experience of doing it will still be there. The experience of the doer will be there – if you like it or not. And then there will be doership. The experience will be there, but the experience doesn't make you the experiencer. There's a phantom with doership and there's no-phantom. This paradox has to be there. And by doing nothing is done, but still something has been done.

So, just stay where no one can stay. Just be what-you-cannot-not-be. I can only repeat that. And That what you cannot-not-be, no one can do because there's no doer. And where there's a doer, there will be doing. And there will be a story of doership. But That what-you-cannot-not-be, there's no doer, so there's no story. So, it's all his-story, the story of the body, the story of consciousness. It's his-story but not your story. But the story continues as there's no bridge between that and That, you cannot have an influence on that whatever is in the movie.

But the last sentence is the best in *Yogavashishta* – see you next time. That's the finishing touch.

Q [Another visitor]: It's in the middle of the book... [Laughter]

K: Doesn't matter. I never read it, so I don't have to know that. That's the best pointer ever – see you next time. All the precious insights, all the teachings and all the so-called profound knowledge, is worth nothing. So, see you next time because whatever you realize now, you have to lose it again.

Q [Another visitor]: When the movie is going on, can I identify the screen?

K: If you're lucky, if it's meant to be, then the reference point of the screen will be your reference point. If the totality wants That to be your reference point, then totality, in your case would experience you from the reference point of awareness. If not, you have to experience yourself from the reference point of your dick. [Laughter]

Q: Or something else...

K: Or something else, but mostly from your dick. Because your dick is your dictator in that reference point. Everyone thinks this [pointing to the heart] is the dictator. No, it's still dictated by that one.

Perception cannot decide from what reference point or angle it experiences itself – impossible. That's the helplessness of the eye of the God. Or the helplessness of the God or Self. It cannot decide from what reference point or point of view, it should perceive itself – impossible. There's no 'willy' in perception. There's not even a need of deciding. There's no one who compares what's a better reference point.

Only from the reference point of a human, there are comparisions. Then you compare the point of views, from your point of view or my point of view. But already in the vertical spirit, there is no comparision. Comparision only happens in the relative – horizontal or human or personal point of views. Then you can compare. Already in vertical there is no comparision, there is knowing. In no time, you cannot compare.

Q [Another visitor]: Knowing or not-knowing...

K: But still it's different from comparision. The non-comparision is different from comparision, so it's relative. A relative vertical, a relative horizontal, then relative awareness. It's all relative. Relative means it's different from something else. The awareness is different from being unconscious – all of that is relative.

Q: Is it better or not better?

K: From the relative point of view, it's better to be in awareness – you cannot deny. Awareness is more peaceful, than being in the body reference point. The experience of peace – relative peace – is much more intense than in this so-called war of body, of these tendencies, of this world. In comparison to that, awareness is better – I agree. But not good enough, because the advantage that you can reach by awareness, it needs one who needs an advantage – and that's still a disadvantage. Because you're still a relative God, who needs an advantage, who needs an experience of peace to experience peace.

For That Absolute God, which is peace, it doesn't need any experience of peace to be peace. So, for That what-you-are, the horizontal is as good as vertical or what is this screen. And only that is worth being. That is fulfillment in absolute sense – innocence. That innocence of absolute fulfillment cannot be reached by any sense and awareness sense, is still a relative sense. The vertical sense, the horizontal sense, sensing something, but That absolute senser you are, cannot be sensed.

Only to be That what is the *parabrahman*, the absolute dreamer, what is your nature – is fulfillment itself. That, you cannot reach, as you cannot lose it.

Q [Another visitor]: But you can get it?

K: No. Never! How can you get what-you-are? Forget it! For-get-it. Forget it, by being it. Because you will never get it. Because what you get, you have to lose again. You will always shift between different senses – reference points. But none of the reference points where you can land, will be forever.

You can say that the reference point of the awareness is a good landing place. But from the good landing place, as from the other landing places, you depart again. Sooner or later, you have to depart and you will always end up in that horizontal bullshit. You cannot avoid the shit, shit will happen. No shit – shitlessness. But out of the shitlessness comes no-shit and shit.

You have to be what-you-are in that *chit* – That which is knowledge – in this shit, the no-shit and the shitlessness. Because you are the nature of the shit, the no-shit and the shitlessness. You cannot avoid yourself. No way out! So, be the market, but not in the market.

All those pointers, don't help; by none of them, you become what-you-are. But only by being what-you-cannot-not-be, is absolute fulfillment because there's no one who needs to be fulfilled in the first place. It's a fulfillment, the knowledge which never needs to be known. Because there is neither a knower or not-knower. Never was, never will be.

So, knowledge doesn't need to know. And that what needs to know, or needs a special place – is hell. Hella-lu-jah – There's a you and a me.

Q [Another visitor joking]: That which cannot come and go, has something to do with visa? [Laughter]

K: You need a Master card not Visa. If you have a Master card, you can go everywhere. But if you have a visa card, you have to be improved. Your credit has to be high – credibility.

But still in relative sense, awareness is better than the body experience. So, if you can stay there, good luck! I give a shit, if you ask me. So, all this precious choiceless awareness that is mentioned in the books, is fine, but it's only fine because no one needs it. If you really would need to be there, to be what-you-are, you still would be fucked by yourself in a delusion of a dream.

So, be aware that you don't need to be aware. Be happy that you don't need to be happy. Enjoy, that you don't need to enjoy. All these paradoxes are the pointers to the paradox. Know that you don't have to know. Stay in that knowledge, that you don't have to know – to know. And that one who needs to know, to know – bye bye. It came and it will be gone. But what-you-are, will still be what-it-is.

In Zen they say, what was your face before you were born? No one knows. Stay in That what has no face, no persona, no reference point at all. Neither having nor not-having. Because the root thought is always the owner thought – having or not-having. Even not having is having too much. Owning or not-owning is not the question.

Q [Another visitor]: Neither knowing nor not knowing, but being...

K: Even being is too much. You don't have to be, to be – That's what-you-are. That what has to be, to be, is already too late. It's depending on being. You are when you are and you are not when you are not. You're the presence and you're the absence. But you're not the presence or the absence. But you're the presence when there's presence and you're the absence when there's absence. But you're not the presence and you're not the absence.

You will never know what you are. You are That! You are That, when there's presence, you are the presence. You're the absence when there's the absence. But you're not the presence and you're not the absence. Because if you would be the presence, you would not be the absence. And if you would be the absence, you would not be the presence.

Undecided! Yes and no. In presence, yes, I Am That. In absence, yes, I Am That – but neither. This is absolute *neti-neti* – neither the presence or the absence – you-are. Stay in That what-you-cannot-not-be because you are That which is in the presence and in the absence what-it-is. You don't need a presence to be what-you-are. And you don't need an absence to be what-you-are.

Q [Another visitor]: You're talking to this 'me' but the mind cannot follow...

K: I don't talk to the mind. I talk to That what-is.

Q: The mind wants to grasp, but it cannot.

K: No. It's like a *koan*. This is splitting the idea of a second because in that no-second, the mind cannot exist. So, it's like creating a paradox in which mind tries, but there's nothing to get. And when there's nothing to get, the mind collapses. And then it wakes up again and tries again. All the talks are like Zen *koans* – creating paradoxes and contradictions that the mind cannot follow.

Q [Another visitor]: When you say, I don't talk to the mind…

K: I talk to myself, who never needs to understand.

Q: But that is mind…

K: No. That is what is the mind but it doesn't know mind.

Q: You can call that mind…

K: I don't have to call it anything. The living words, where there's no one speaking, no one listening. That what you can call life which never needs to know life to be life. Which is breaking the idea that life needs to know life to be alive. You can fish and I always make it a bit more mysty – mysterious.

I can only sit here and destroy everything that can be destroyed, even the destroyer gets destroyed. But it's not good enough. So, I always present the failure. You will fail, fail, fail and fail.

Q [Another visitor]: The mind will fail…

K: You will fail. You will never know yourself. I'm talking to That what will always fail because what-you-are will never know itself. And I can just put you into That absolute absence of a knower, because there is no knower. The knower already means knowing – to exist. But that knowledge of existence is already ignorance.

Q: This idea of individual?

K: This idea that you-are. This 'I Am', this first 'I'. To destroy the first root thought 'I' – the first presence. Talking to That what doesn't even need presence – to be what-it-is. That's called the living words which are without any intention.

By trying not to kill you, leaving you, as you are, caring a shit about your presence and absence, talking to what I Am. Because That never needs to be addressed, never needs anything to know or not to know.

I know it's futile, but I try. It's not needed, but I try.

Q [Another visitor]: Thank you for trying... [Laughter]

K: Imagine I would sit by choice talking to you. Imagine, I would have a choice – bye bye. No one would ever see me again.

Q [Another visitor]: It's not so bad Karl...

K: It's worse, I tell you. [Laughter] I would rather stay in bed and watch movies.

Q [Another visitor]: What about caring for other people?

K: Shit happens! [Laughter]

Q: So, is it always their responsibility or do I have to care what I do?

K: You have to care. But don't care that you care. If you have a mother, you have to care about your mother. If you have a girlfriend, a collegue, you have to care. You better care. What else to do? When you drive on streets, you have to drive on the right side. There's a natural caring.

Q: I meant it in an emotional way. You can live your life like you want to live it. You fuck around and hurt people and think it's their life...

K: Yeah. Fuck them all! [Laughter] I say it, but I don't do it. But if you ask me, from the understanding, I would fuck them all.

Q: So, it's part of their experience?

K: It's your experience but it's their exprience too. It's an experience of what-you-are. You cannot hurt anybody.

Q: I'm not sure. I care a little bit... [Laughter]

K: If you are conscious about what you do and you care, then you better don't do things that are bad for others. But you have to do it anyway. You will hurt somebody – if you like it or not. And you have to leave people and connect again and you hurt people, if you like it or not.

So, even in the relative sense, you cannot avoid it. No one can stay pure and not hurt anyone. Even St. Francis of Assisi, one of the biggest sages, had to go to the Pope and tell him that he was doing something wrong. He was hurting the pope. And he was hurting everyone who was bad more than anybody else, because he was too good to be true. The good people are hurting everyone around them. Because everyone feels bad around them.

I actually like more the bad people than the good people. I like people who hurt people because then people feel free to hurt them. [Laughter] If you're someone who doesn't hurt anybody, the other already feels hurt by you – because you're too good to be true. No one actually believes you anyway – impossible.

Things will happen anyway. You will hurt and you will be hurt. That's the way it is – pain is there. The misery you cannot stop. Actually in this relative realm, there's only misery. You can only give misery and take misery and get miserable. This is a realm of – me's. And where there are me's acting, there's misery. It's all misery. That's why it's called hell. The human hell. What humans can do to humans, even the devil cannot invent. How cruel people can be to each other and to themselves. That's why it's called hell. And you cannot stop it.

If you as the almighty – whatever almighty means, the omnipotence of God – cannot stop it and cannot change it, even he is impotent of stopping this cruelty of humanity – Who do you think you are? We have to bear with Angela Merkel. [Laughter] Now she's in Greek papers as the Hitler.

You cannot dream what happens. You cannot imagine that things like that could happen again. There was no day in humanity when there was no war on earth and one killing the other. And it will never stop – out of love. So, the dream that by the end of this year, there will be the end of all this drama – nice dream. We will see.

Q: I'm not sure...

K: I believe too that it will continue as it is. No way out of this hell of humanity, killing each other. But sooner or later, humanity will be gone anyway. We shouldn't worry so much about it. Human consciousness is just a period in the entire timescale. It's like a disease, one day consciousness will be healed from humanity. [Laughing]

But then it comes back – that's the problem. Some other kind of Klingon world will happen. [Laughter]

Q [Another visitor]: It's not philosophy, the sun will one day explode...

K: Yeah. Sooner or later, there will be no sun. There was a time when there was no sun and there will be a time when there will be no sun. It's like God inhaling and everything is destroyed and then it exhales and everything is created – again and again – as it was before. Inhaling – taking everything back and exhaling – creating again as it is now.

How many times did you do that? Destroy the whole universe in a single [inhaling]. But at that moment you forgot how it was and then [exhaling] – Oh look, something happened. Ramana gave the example of a spider trying to catch itself in its own web. And maybe sooner or later, it realizes that it cannot catch itself in its own web. So, by realizing that it cannot catch itself in its own web, it withdraws the whole web [inhaling]. But then when the spider does not know any spider, what does the spider do in his glorious, spiderless existence? Just by accident, waking up. And what's the nature of the spider? Spinning.

It's like a mind. What's the nature of a mind? Spinning, fucking, minding itself, minding the mind. And this is all minding the mind.

So, never mind. It will happen again – again and again. And nothing to gain in – again and again mind-fuck. Existence penetrating itself, vibrating in infinite possible ways and possibilities. Fucking itself in an imaginary fuck. Being an imaginary fucker fucking an imaginary fuck. An imaginary lover, an imaginary dick – *lingam* – creates an imaginary space. And then the *lingam* vibrates in the imaginary space creating all the suns and all the universes by all the vibrations. This is all the vibration of light of that what is life. And then the *lingam* just stops again. And by stopping, the whole universe stops – in silence.

Q: Only the one sun goes...

K: No. All the suns go in the black hole.

Q: The sun has lived five billion years and has another twenty five and then it explodes...

K: We will talk later when that happens. [Laughter]

We're all vibrators of existence and every morning this little *lingam* wakes up – what a dick! When you turn off the electricity, it goes back to sleep. And one day there will be a power cut – no Karl anymore. That's when you call Karl's dead – a little power cut. If there's no re-animation somewhere from outside – bye bye – as if nothing ever happened. So, it's already now! And all the precious blah, blah, blah that this body can do, will be [blowing in the wind] puffed forever – in to the blue.

February 10, 2012. Evening Talk.
Thailand

Even oneness is fascism because it claims to be better than separation

Q: I feel very stupid...

K: That's actually your nature. You can only feel stupidity, so you felt stupid. Knowledge cannot be felt, so you can only feel stupidity. If you feel dumb, you're more in your natural state.

Q: Yesterday I didn't feel good...

K: Why?

Q: I didn't follow what was going on. I didn't understand it anymore. Now I've booked for all the sessions [Laughter]. Now I don't have to worry anymore, should I leave or not...

K: [Mocking] Whether I stay or not – who cares? The ride is paid. It's like your funeral is already paid, the tombstone is already finished. Now you can wait until it happens. It's like you're in a carousel, now it's too late to leave. It will stop when it stops. You paid your entrance – you are born. Your tombstone is already engraved. You already have a 'Rest In Peace' in front of your forehead – nothing to worry anymore. What else to do?

Q [Another visitor]: Can you look at the news without being upset? When J. Krishnamurti saw the killing of whales on television, he switched off the television...

K: Maybe that's one solution. [Laughter] I can watch it, but sometimes in the United States I get pissed because it's obviously stupid. Anyone in a bad mood about the world? If not yet, we can work on it. [Laughter]

Q [Another visitor]: If you don't see it, you're not in a bad mood.

K: Even then you get in a bad mood because you're surrounded by people who saw it. You get the news – watch it! [Laughter] If you're not interested, whoever is around you is interested and he will tell you inspite of you wanting to hear it or not. You cannot escape.

People try to go to Himalayas and become hermits, and they cannot. Then even a small fly disturbs them. You will be disturbed – if you like it or not.

Q [Another visitor]: One is complaining intellectually about America, one is complaining about the government and the other one is complaining about the body...

K: The complainer wakes up in the morning – the worrier – and then he starts to complain. That is his duty, his job. He's never plain enough, he has to come-plain. It's either too boring or too much is happening. Nothing happening is not good, too much happening is not good, and the middle is not good. You will find something – don't worry.

Worry and be happy because the worries happen by themselves and then complaining happens anyway.

Q: It's like, come we can play...

K: Yeah. Let's play complainer. That's why everyone asks – How are you? And then he wants to hear a complaint.

Q: What was your dream last night? [Laughter] I answered a lady in America and I thought she was really interested...

K: No. No one is interested. He's there only to get rid of his own shit, but not to hear other's shit – vomiting it out. Then he gets rid of it and you have to take it home. [Laughter]

I have fun in States, when they ask me – How are you today? I say I'm very bad – and they already turn away. They say – I love you and I say – Yes, I hate you too. And then they start laughing because they see the joke. They know it's bullshit. You have to make fun about it.

Life is shit – moment-by-moment.

Q [Another visitor]: When there's higher shit, it smells good, when you're in lower shit, it doesn't feel so good...

K: When you're in the shit, you don't smell the shit anymore. If you're on top of the shit, you smell it. If you want to be separated from the shit, then you really smell the shit.

Q: Sometimes the smell of the shit is okay when you are far away...

K: But then you have to come closer again.

Q: For what?

K: To smell the shit because you have to go to the toilet sooner and later. It's all your own shit and being in the shit, you don't know any shit. So you better be the shit itself. Shit doesn't mind shit. But if you're different from shit, then you're in trouble. When you're not shit, then you're in trouble. For me, all is shit. Whatever is, is shit, shit, shit...

Q: Is shit and life same?

K: Yeah. The opposite of live is evil – it's all evil. The moment you experience life, you experience hell – evil.

Q: And you experience heaven?

K: Even heaven belongs to hell because only in hell, there's two. In heaven there would be no hell – if there would be a heaven, but heaven is an idea, as hell is an idea. Only in the idea of hell, there's heaven, both come together. So, both is hell – Hellalujah! Hello – it's very low.

So, if everything is hell, who cares? Only when you have this idea that you can get out of hell, then you're in trouble. When you are the devil in hell, you're fine. When you want to be an angel in hell, then you're an health angel.

No. Being shit, seeing shit – it's fine. No way out of shit, because shit cannot leave shit. If the shit wants to be a special shit, it's really shitty. Then the organic people, they don't want to stink. It's like an *ashram* – shit goes in and compost comes out. [Laughter] These esoteric organic assholes, trying to become better than the rest of the world. These fascistic ideas – that something has to be changed.

I always like to call esoteric people as fascists. I mean it. Hitler was the biggest esoteric asshole I know. The Thule people from Aryas are the biggest esoteric community on earth – crazy. In Japan too, the rising sun, the dark sun and all those esoteric ideas. Zen is fascism.

Whatever is – is fascism. Every intention, every religion, every movement is all fascistic. Even oneness is fascism because oneness claims to be better than separation, so it's fascism. Heaven is fascism, God is fascism. All the angels are fascistic soldiers. Now we have a German pope, it's now very clear – it's all fascism. I'm German, I know what is fascism. Germans always know how it could be better.

And I always like to call Eckhart Tolle a fascist. [Laughter]

Q [Another visitor]: Why?

K: The new earth is the most fascistic idea.

Q: Why? It's for everybody, it's not just for him...

K: Because he knows what's best for everybody – that's fascism. Every good person has a good intention, but any intention is fascistic.

Q: And what about you sitting here?

K: I'm a fascist myself. I talk about myself. I'm the true fascist.

[Laughter, clapping] I don't take myself out of the game, I always know better than anybody else how it has to be. It's always a competition of fascism. Who's the biggest fascist? So, what to do if you cannot escape it? Even not to be a fascist is fascism. If you say fascism is not good, I'm an anti-fascist – I'm more fascist than a fascist. Fascistic asshole I am – fantastic!

[Pointing to a visitor] She brought a fascist to me. She had a patient who was a television producer who made anti-fascistic movies. He came and one lady said that in Tiruvannamalai you always said everything is fascistic. And he started saying – That's not true, you cannot say that, I forbid you to say that. I said look now the fascist wakes up. He said, you cannot call me a fascist, my father was a fascist and I fought fascism my entire life. I told him you're bigger than your father. Then he took his money back and wanted to leave with his wife. But his wife said, No. I like it. [Laughter] And six months later they were divorced.

Q: [Laughter] And you were guilty...

K: This story I hear very often. They come as a couple and a bit later I hear that they're not together anymore. It seems like when they come, suddenly they have the courage to kick the ass of the other. Before they were all afraid that they will lose something by losing someone. Suddenly they see that they have nothing to lose – fuck off, leave me alone. So, it's dangerous to come here. After a while, they're all single. [Laughter] Otherwise they really had to fight for their so-called relationship. They get so tired after the talk that they cannot fight any more. They say – okay, piss off, just go.

Q [Another visitor]: So, every thought, every idea is fascistic?

K: The whole world is fascism. If I ask you – How are you? And I want to know and I want to help you – it's fascism. It's all good intention but it's all fascism. Good intention, bad intention is all fascism.

Q: When you say the duality comes out of good intention...

K: Already God is the first fascist.

Q: Fascism means good intention?

K: Yes. Now there are seven billion ideas of what is good. So, out of the idea of good comes good intention. But from every position, point of view, everyone is honest. Even Bush and Hitler had good intention but from their reference point. So, every reference point fights against the other reference point. Even in a relationship, two reference points fighting for a good relationship. Everyone has a good intention, but sometime they kill each other – out of good intention.

Q: That's where it seems a bit unbelievable...

K: Why? But it's very obvious.

Q: Everyone is fighting for peace...

K: Yeah. Everyone is fighting for good intention and the intention is always happiness or peace. Even religions – they kill each other – for good, for their God, for their idea of goodness. My God is better than your God, my goodness is better than your goodness. My God is more almighty than your almighty God. Both are almighty, but mine is more almighty than yours. More holy – for sure and stronger. Fantastic!

Q: It's a very strong hypnosis...

K: It's not hypnosis, it's just good intention. But as you see yourself in this world of infinite positions and points of views, from every angle there's good intention – good intention fighting good intention. So, there's a war of good intention. You cannot find any bad intention. Whoever you ask, every soldier fights for peace. So, everyone fights for peace. There's fighting for peace, looking for harmony.

But because you want to create harmony, it should be your harmony, your way, from your point of view. Then you fight for it and you really think you are right, because you are God and God is always right. If this is the position of God, God fights for his right and that's the natural insight of everybody that they're right.

It has to be like this. Everyone is totally convinced that this is the right point and I mean it well. It's like a father beating up his son. It's only for your good. It hurts me more than you, but I have to do it for good of our family.

Q: When you say it like that, it seems very clear...

K: It is clear.

Q: Thank you... [Laughter]

K: And every teacher is the same. Every guru, from his position, his reference point, the I Amness or Awareness or beyond, he says all of the rest is shit, only my position is right. I found the reference point which is true. I found truth. I realized truth. Now I tell the rest of the world that everybody else is wrong. So, he fights from that position because he really believes that it is the truth and everyone else is wrong. If he finds someone similar, then okay – maybe he has a good point, but my point is a little bit better.

Q [Another visitor]: Are you saying any thought, any point of view is...

K: Any intention, any idea...

Q: It's all fascism in expression?

K: Any word is a fascistic expression.

Q: So, it's only beyond words that...

K: Even that is fascism.

Q: You're saying that it is not possible to find truth in words?

K: The moment you pronounce it, it's fascism – comes out of fascism.

Q: Even if I say 'unpronounceable', the Absolute that's unpronounced...

K: Is fascist! The Absolute fascist! I mean it. The intention out of goodness is good intention. But that's already fascism.

Q: But that's not the Absolute...

K: It is the Absolute. That where all the intention comes from, all the dream, all what-is – is the dream of the Absolute. It's an Absolute dream of fascism. The fascism is not negative, don't take it negative. For me it's not negative. It's good intention to know yourself. All of that comes from God trying to know himself, dreaming inquiring into himself. Trying to imagine itself, it's the imagination of the 'I' and then imagining what one can be or not – what God is. How can he not? That's the way he realizes himself. So, he becomes a fascist.

It's natural. It's the nature of realization, realizing himself and you always want to have the best – that's love. Love is fascism because love is good intention. Love means I only want to have the best for myself – good intention and goodness would be the best. So, love makes you a fascist. Love creates fascism and everything comes out of love – out of good intention. So, everything is fascism.

You cannot make Absolute separate from the realization of the Absolute. The realization of Reality, is Reality. The nature of realization, is Reality. So, it's an absolute realization of absolute love which is fascism, because love means good intention. For me fascism is not right or wrong, it's just the way it is and you cannot escape it. It's not that I'm saying Hitler was a good guy, or others were as bad as him.

No! There's no badness, there's only goodness and fascism is the intention of goodness – the intention to know yourself and to realize yourself. You sit here out of fascism because you want to have the best for yourself. Or you want to have the worse? But if you want to have the worse, that is because you think it would be better.

Q: Yeah. That's the motivation...

K: The motivation is always good. Even a masochist has an idea of total pain because he thinks from total pain he can gain something, that he gains peace. For me words are never negative, I just use them as they are there. If I say shit, for me shit is nothing negative. Shit is just a word like goodness or anything else. There's no taste of it.

Q: What do you mean by there's no taste of it?

K: Normally when you say shit, the others think you better don't say anything dirty. It's your conditioning that shit is not so good or fuck is not so good. For me it's all just empty words, empty bullshit words.

Q: The living words...

K: You are the living asshole there. [Silence] You see!

And that I like about UG [Krishnamurti]. He used words like piece of cake or coffee. There are no bad words. It's just a conditioning of your fucking mother or your father – whoever tells you that you have to put soap in your mouth because you said a f-word. Bullshit. It's because they're afraid to do it.

So much bullshit happening, but you cannot avoid it. All this conditioning and moralistic condoms were put over you. The words are dirty and you should not say this and you should not do this and blah, blah, blah. Religions are like daily rules of how to survive. But there's nothing that you can gain for your eternal life or something. Over our shoulder is all this genetic bullshit of our ancestors. In that moment it may have been right but now it's so much bullshit. Don't bite into the apple. But now everyone bites the apple. No one learnt anything.

Q [Another visitor]: If I understood you, your idea of fascism is same as the idea of separation. Is it?

K: Trying to overcome separation is just a trip. It's a fascistic intention. But trying to overcome separation confirms separation. So, the intention of goodness, makes things bad. The intention of good means, goodness has to come. It's not there. So, any good intention already makes this moment bad because goodness is not here.

Q: And you want something better?

K: Yeah. First you have to confirm that this is not good. Then by trying to make it better, you confirm that it's all a shit. It is shit. But what you get will be shit too. You take the experience of separation as real and from there on you want to overcome it, you want to change it. The good intention of trying to get rid of separation or going to oneness – confirms separation. The trap is absolutely perfect.

As absolute you-are, as absolute is your ignorance.

Q: And the ignorance of the world, of all the *gurus*?

K: It's a result of it. Out of the ignorance of God, ignorant *gurus* appear. Ignorant disciples, ignorant *gurus*, all whatever comes from the first awareness – God knowing himself is ignorance. So, any knowing is ignorance. God knowing God is already two Gods – is ignorance. It's a dream of knowing, all dream and all misunderstanding. Any understanding is a misunderstanding – Any!

So, any understanding is shit. Even understanding that every understanding is shit – is shit. Shit, shit shit! And I like it. You cannot escape the shit because you are the shit. *Sat-shit-ananda*. It will never end. The never ending shit. That's the new title of my book – The never ending shit. [Laughter]

Q: Is imagination only a function of consciousness?

K: Imagination is already a result that there is one who's in shit. Now you try to imagine how it would be without shit, without separation. That's the false evidence that you as an experiencer is separate from what you experience – the imagination starts. Then you try to imagine yourself being out of it. You try to imagine truth because you think this cannot be true. And you are right! This cannot be real.

The experience of separation cannot be real, by intuition you know that. Then you try to imagine how to end that. Out of the false, you create an imagination of how can I get out of the false.

Because by intuition, by heart you know that this cannot be true. This is not it. This is a knowledge that this cannot be true. But from that moment on, you fall in love with yourself, you try to find the real love, because this relative love cannot be it.

So, you are missing yourself by knowing yourself – instantly. And by missing yourself, you are in the misery of missing – being one who is missing himself. Then you imagine how to get out of that missing? How to get out of that misery? It's natural and the good intention is that I want to have the best for myself, know myself, realizing myself as That what I Am. But from then on, you have to separate yourself from what you experience.

Then you meditate on yourself and try to be in that space where you can only be That what is real. So, you separate yourself from this – instantly. By imagining yourself out of it, you become arrogant – apart God.

Q: I imagine myself getting results or not getting results...

K: You don't want this, that you know. But you don't know what you want. So, you imagine something what would be better than this. Because you don't want this.

Q: And everything I imagine, is missing it...

K: It's too late – because now there is one God and by existing he's missing That what is his nature. Nature doesn't exist, but the moment you exist, you are missing That what-you-are.

Q: Stuck in an imagination...

K: Then you try to imagine nature of yours. But whatever you imagine, is an image of your... It's not what you are. Already this is an imagination, but by already trying to end this imagination, you create another image of yourself. So, the false creates false. It starts false and it creates false. False, false, false, false, false – everywhere. Here, there and beyond – false, false, false. Whatever you imagine – is false.

But how to end that? Trying to end it – is false. The phantom is 'I' and 'I' will I-magine. The false trying not to be false. The unreal trying not be unreal – trying to become real. That's his bloody nature. Consciousness trying to know consciousness. Consciousness already is unreal. Then consciousness tries to know consciousness – penetrating consciousness. A phantom penetrating a phantom and creating other phantoms – infinite phantoms, more and more phantoms. Now there are seven billion Adams and Eves, Kane and Able and all of that – coming out of that first Adam, which is already false.

Q [Another visitor]: The story of eating the apple. Did Adam and Eve try to escape permanent separation?

K: Adam had a choice – tree of knowledge or tree of life and the tree of life was to bite the apple. He made a wrong choice. He went outwards not inwards. The tree of life would be eternal life – which is turning to God, turning to that knowledge he is. All happened because Adam wanted the tree of life – I Am – the lady was waiting. The lady is the *yoni* – space. The *lingam* didn't choose to be That what is the *lingam*, the tree of knowledge, he chose the tree of life – the I Amness. And now we see the result of it.

All the polarities and all that shit, all the 'I'-pods. [Laughter]

Q: Now you cannot escape the polarities?

K: Now it's too late. The choice happened. What to do? That's why I say – It's too late now – the choice happened.

Q: Is it in the evolution of mankind, the brain gets bigger so that the thoughts do not separate and we live one with the animals?

K: Animals live separate too. Why would the animals not separate? Does an ant embrace an elephant?

Q: They are not judging...

K: By nature they judge. A monkey eats a banana and not whatever.

Q: But they don't feel guilty about it...

K: Who knows? Can you remember how you were as a monkey? An elephant remembers you if you step on his feet for hundred years. There will be revenge. Consciousness as a monkey is as stupid as a human. Everyone thinks that the animal kingdom has more innocence. You think a lion eats meat because it's just his nature to eat meat. But if a guy shoots me on the street, it's not his nature, it's by intention because he has a free-will.

No! There is no free-will in both of them. Both are just consciousness playing fucking funny. This little idea that humans have freewill – they have a willy but not freewill. No one can want what he wants – not even a human, not even God can want what he wants.

Q: How do you know?

K: Try to want what you want before you want what you want. Try it! People ask me how can I stop thinking? Try to think before you think what you think. Stop! Nothing comes. Or try to think in Mongolian. It's very easy to stop the mind.

Q: But you are talking about God...

K: I am talking about God because [pointing to the visitor] there is God sitting claiming to be stupid. And trying to know himself. Who else is here? Fucking God! Show me anyone who is not God. In his bullshit action. And if even in his first moment of waking up he cannot avoid waking up...

Q: This is not God, this is a creation of God...

K: No! This is God in action. So, it's God in bullshit God.

Q: It's God too...

K: It's not God too – it's all God, in action and in no-action. The presence and the absence of God. But the nature of God is neither the presence of God or the absence of God, because the nature of God doesn't know any God. But the moment God knows God – like here – God is stupid like hell and by trying to get out of this hell of ignorance, he becomes a devil – the Be-God [bigot].

Q: In our mind...

K: Not in your mind. You think you have a mind? Look at how arrogant God becomes – he claims that he has a mind [Laughter] and then 'our' mind. You see how God can pronounce bullshit? He even claims that he has a mind. He even claims that he has a religion. He claims – becomes a claimer. How stupid can God be that he claims something he already owns? He is the Absolute owner of what-is. But now he claims to have a little body and he sees other Gods who have other bodies. Then he's fucking irritated that he is a God having a body and there's another God there – What am I doing? I thought I'm the only God. Why are there so many Gods now? I have to fight them all.

You're just playing stupid – that's all. And why not? There's nothing to lose in it – playing clever, playing stupid, playing ignorant. It's all a play anyway. I sit here to remind you – Come on, it's just a play. My Goodness! Did something happen? In your whole so-called existence, did something happen? You are still that perception – unspoiled, untainted. As you were even before Adam and Eve appeared. Since then nothing ever happened, because your nature is untainted, unchanged – by anything.

None of these whatever events of the world, of the universe, and the suns and things, never altered your nature. So, you can be stupid as hell – Who cares? It doesn't make you stupid, experiencing yourself as stupid and playing stupid. That what is playing itself as stupid is not stupid by playing stupid. It just plays stupid. You always do 'as-if'.

I don't want to change it. I have no intention to change anything. I can just point – Look at it! Be what-you-cannot-not-be and enjoy the play because this is one way of playing and it's as good or as bad as the other way of playing. Playing this body, playing this life of Karl is as good or as bad as any bloody life of any bloody elephant or ant or any bloody whoever.

It's stupid, but the question is – What to do? You try every possible way to end that bullshit, but trying to end the bullshit is part of the play. So, even that is cheating yourself – but who cares of being cheated by oneself? No one else can cheat you as you can cheat yourself. You are the trapper, the trapping and the trapped – in persona. The Absolute persona trapping itself in a relative persona. Who else can make you believe that you have a bloody body as you can make yourself believe in that bullshit?

There's no mother who can do that, there's no father, there's no conditioning. If you would not do what you do to yourself, no one else can do that to you. In the form of your mother, in the form of your father, in the form of your whole world – you betray yourself. But being betrayed by yourself, who fucking cares?

It's the same as television. This is your tell-lie-vision. You are the Absolute liar and you always tell yourself lies. It's all tell-lie-vision. The whole experiences of the lies of universe – is lies. You are the only watcher – the eye of God and this is your own program – Buddha's television set. Not so bad, but not so good because you cannot change the program. [Laughter]

But now you think you have to change the program because you feel bored, you became a seeker. You want to have a different program. You want to have a truth program, that has Gangaji on it. [Laughter] But after a while, you get more bored than ever. Then you switch back to the action movie. [Laughter] The holy program becomes very boring, the unlimited – Pope in different personas. [Mocking] You have to make a new earth and Oprah Winfrey tells you that world can only be safe by being transformed in to a higher consciousness – blah, blah, blah. It really sounds like a new church. Fantastic!

How much bullshit can God do? Unlimited! As unlimited is his nature, as unlimited is his shit.

Q: You say be-what-you-cannot-not-be. For me it's easier to say be-what-you-cannot-be...

K: Be-what-you-cannot-not-be, and as you are That already what is Reality already, you have to realize yourself as a 'me' – you cannot avoid it. You have to experience yourself as a realizer – a creator that is different from his creation. You cannot otherwise. This is the way you realize yourself. That's the 'me'.

Q: In other language I cannot say that – not-not. You can say be-what-you-cannot-be...

K: How can you not be That – what-you-cannot-not-be? [Laughter] That stops you in an instant. That's a *koan* you cannot break. The knower stops. The knower, the knowing, what can be known stops – in one instant.

Ramana always said – Be-what-you-are. Instantly there's this question – How? But if you say be-what-you-cannot-be, for whatever a split-second there's silence. And for sure, something pops in, but it takes a while. Sometimes longer, sometimes shorter. That's the *neti-neti*. It's like a *koan* which cannot be broken by the mind. Whatever then remains – the eye of God, the silence – there's no problem. But then the mind pops up again and tries to make it a concept, for sure.

Q: I cannot be That, I cannot be That, and the mind stops again...

K: Yeah.

Q: Then there's the other not...

K: The other not is erasing the 'not' – not-not. It came out of a circumstance when someone was asking about Ramana's – Be-what-you-are. He said, there's an instant question – How? Then I said, okay try be-what-you-cannot-not-be. Then there was this blankness. I said, okay, it works. This was not by invention, it just came out of a moment. It was created by itself. So, I cannot even say – I created that.

It's like Ramana's renunciation of renunciation. It's the same, coming out of a necessity of the moment. He had to do it because he was in a court and they wanted to take away his *ashram* because in India a sadhu cannot own anything. So, he could not own the *ashram*, someone wanted to take the land and he had to go to the court. Ramana said, I even renounce renunciation, so I can own again. By renouncing renunciation, owning is not an obstacle. And then it was invented. That became his biggest saying and I like it the most.

Renouncing the renouncing, in That the renouncer cannot be found. The devotion of devotion – what is that? That's *neti-neti* again. The *bhakti* of *bhakti* – be the *bhakti* of *bhakti*. Be the *jñani* of the *jñani* – who doesn't know any *jñani*. It's all negative-negative – erasing of the relative whatever you imagine to be – but all out of what? The totality creates it out of the blue, but not by calculating. [Mocking] What can I now say to my disciples that makes them stop their mind?

No! It's all totality in action. As many traps God creates, as many loop holes he creates to that – whatever.

Q [Another visitor]: Why do people lie down and pass out during your talks?

K: Because they get very exhausted trying to follow it.

Q: So, by tying the knots to the mind...

K: I exhaust them. That's what I can do. I exhaust what they believe to be. In that total exhaustion, some lie down, some get whatever. But in that exhaustion of ideas, what-you-are remains – as what-it-is. Everyone comes here to get exhausted and not to get refreshed. [Laughter] This is not a refreshment party or a wellness club.

I can never exhaust That what I-am, that I show, but they try to become That and in That they get exhausted. And by trying to exhaust what-it-is – That never needs to be what-it-is – is just That. That's the effortlessness of – That. There's no effort needed for you to be what-you-cannot-not-be. But That what-you-are-not, by trying to become That, you get exhausted. Because all the concepts of what you can try, what you can be – you really try but it's too much. That's why they call me a sleeping pill. [Laughter] Some call me a sleeping pill. They go to bed and cannot sleep. Then they listen to me for fifteen minutes and then they wake up in a loop with my voice after eight hours. Crazy! I would fall asleep listening to myself instantly, as I do all the time.

No. It's like resistance to That makes you tired. But resistance is futile because what-you-are already wants to get rid of that whatever is resisting. That they call grace. If the Self again wants to be That what-you-cannot-not-be, it shows no mercy to the body in front of it. And it will be exhausted and the mind will be exhausted. All of that will be exhausted, sooner or later – if you like it or not.

It's like a call back to home. The father calls you home, but you don't want to go. You want to play a bit longer.

[Interruption by a bee flying around]

That was a bee, I thought it was a fly. That's like you want to play but it's something that will sting you. The poison is now working since the first gift of Osho or whatever ideas came to you and now the spirit has already turned around and you need a lot of effort to turn the spirit to the world. You try very hard but it doesn't work anymore and then when you turn to that what is silence, you get tired and by trying to resist it, you get even more tired. So, it's not in your hand. You will be assimilated. [Laughter] If you like it or not. Resistance is futile.

Sooner or later you will be assimilated too, because this [pointing to the body] will be assimilated, it will die. You will be without it anyway – if you like it or not. So, now clinging on to this [body] and thinking that this has to live longer and I don't want to die and all of that, is anyway bullshit.

Q [Another visitor]: So, what-you-are is effortlessness, but the personality is the effort...

K: It wants to survive. It's like the phantom tendencies of this body want to survive. You want to live forever as what you think you are, but it's not possible. You cannot survive – but you try. You eat organic, you go to wellness clubs, you do enema, you try your best to live longer. Actually you don't like to live, but you want to live longer. [Laughter] It's crazy! [Mocking] Maybe it gets better. Maybe it's a precious possibility. And teachers tell you this is a precious life, and a precious possibility that you can realize yourself – in this life!

Q [Another visitor]: We fear that in next life we come as a monkey...

K: You fear the monkey and that makes you a monkey. You become a monk looking for a key of heaven – that makes you a monkey. And then you have the key of heaven and you knock, but then there's no one at home! You have a key and you can even open the door. But when you look, there's no one there. This bloody God is never at home because he went out and now he thinks that he needs a key to go back home.

Then you go back to that absence – no one there. Shit! I better go back where someone is. Then you come back here and say – There was no one. [Laughter] There is nobody, you better stay here and have a little fun. First you have to go through all the arch angels – Hello! Hello! But no one at home.

Q [Another visitor]: What is the ark of the covenant?

K: In the movie Indiana Jones, they showed it like a nuclear reactor – when you look at it, you die. It's like when you look at the eye of God, you die. If you open that secret box, you will not survive as you imagine to be. That's the symbol of, if you look at the essence of life, you cannot survive. If you look at That what is the truth, you will be gone. Actually it's a synonym of enlightenment. When you look into That what is light, there's no one who can take it. You can only be the light, but no one can take the light. That's the symbol.

You cannot take truth, you cannot know truth because the moment you look into truth, you are gone. There's no truth, there's no one who can know truth. But when you look at the truth, that one who sees truth – dissolves – instantly. That's called the split-second – you cannot take it. No one could ever take it. When there's truth, there's no one – never was, never will be – because there's no two.

That's what Ramana said to UG [Krishnamurti] when he asked – Can you give it to me? Yes! But can you take it? The moment you look, you're gone. You wouldn't have anything from it. You cannot have it. You cannot claim to have it. And whoever claims that he realized truth, is an asshole. There was never anyone who realized truth. In truth, there's no truth.

Q: You cannot talk about it?

K: You can talk about it, but there's no one who can claim it. It cannot be owned and you cannot put it in your pearls of memory. [Mocking] Now I looked into truth, now I want to share the pearl – bullshit! It's for no one. No one can have it.

Q: It's very powerful – this symbol...

K: Whatever you try is to look away from it because you are afraid that you cannot take it. And you're right, you cannot take it. Even meditating is closing the eyes for it. You always try not to see it, but sometimes it's unavoidable, so you cannot resist. So, your system collapses and then it cannot be avoided anymore. There's no tendency or energy left to avoid it and then it takes you. [Sucking the air in] But you cannot take the truth, truth takes you.

Grace eats you up, but you cannot be in grace. In grace, no one can be. In grace, even the idea of grace drops because you are the idea of grace. And if the Self wants to be the Self, the Self drops the idea of Self – in one instant, without any hesitation. And only That what is the Self can drop the idea of Self. But not this little bullshit 'me' who thinks that now by the little understanding, it can drop something and devote something. No one needs your bloody devotion. What is yours anyway what you could devote?

Your bloody *bhakti* – Fuck thee! [Laughter] In Bavarian, *bhakti* means piss-off. That's the symbol in Jewish Karbalah. In another religion, it's the box of Pandora.

Q [Another visitor]: In Pandora's box when you open the box there's hope...

K: Yeah. And hope is hell, so you look into the hell and see that it will never die. When you see hope will never die, that's truth. Inquiry will never stop because the hope will never die. The love for yourself will never stop and there will never be any fulfillment because the hope will never stop. That you can call truth because in that you cannot survive. How can you survive without hope?

Hope will never stop. So, the phantom will never die. That's the truth. Consciousness will never stop looking for consciousness. And in That you cannot survive as a 'me'. You can only survive in the hope that one day it will be over. But it will never be over. So, that's the Pandora's box.

Q: The woman opens the box and all the curses for the mankind were unleashed...

K: What is a woman? Hope! Maybe the translation was wrong, someone translated academically. A good hope is a pregnant woman. That's why they call it a woman in good hope. That there will be a child who will end this drama – a Messiah! This is a good hope. That there will be a son of God. That God will come to earth and end this drama.

But he will never come. He cannot come! Because he's already here – this asshole. How can he come? How can there be a son of God? What do they say in Jewish? There can never be any son of God – no Messiah. That's the pointer that the hope for it keeps it going. The Messiah may come and every woman may carry the new Messiah. So, that's the good hope. And the next child will be the deliverance of God – blah, blah, blah. Maybe it was Eckhart Tolle and we didn't see it. [Laughter]

That's why I always hit on anyone who gives you this hope, because this is hell and that keeps you in this bullshit. But I try and I know that it doesn't work. [Laughter] Now you have a hope of 'no hope'. Just changing the direction – nothing works! But then you say, maybe that works.

The tricks to escape are infinite. But maybe one day the box of tricks is empty.

Q [Another visitor]: December 21, 2012…

K: December 22. You are one day too early – missed again! [Laughter]

Q [Another visitor]: So, you use hope in the sense Buddha used desire and said that's what kept the whole thing going, the hope that one day the desire would end…

K: Yeah. He tried forty years to end desire, in the end he had to say – I failed, I'm the absolute failure. I tried all possible ways to end desire – the hope. And without hope there cannot be any desire because only in hope you do something, you desire what comes out of hope. It didn't work. So, he resigned in a way from the idea that he can ever know himself. Because that would mean he could end desire. The desiring of himself will never end.

The same with Nisargadatta – The Ultimate Medicine means inquiry will never stop, but you can never find the inquirer. The seeking will never stop, but you cannot find the seeker. The ultimate medicine is to see that seeking will never stop. And by seeing that the seeking will never stop, the seeker cannot survive. The seeker can only be there in the hope that one day it will end. But by seeing that it will never end – that is the truth.

Consciousness will always look for consciousness. The ignorance, the unreal will always try to become real. But the unreal will never become real. Where is 'you' in it? You resign from that idea and without the idea that you will ever end, where is the 'me'? Never was there. The 'me' is only the hope that one day it may end – by your doing or not doing. The doership can only be there in the hope or idea that one day by your doing or not doing, or understanding or not understanding, it will end.

So, whatever you try to do is trying to end it. But the truth is that it will never end – as it never started, how can it end? So, what to do? This is the beginning of the end – or is it the end of the beginning? I don't know.

I always talk about the worse case – that you can never end the misery.

Q: This brings hopelessness...

K: Hopelessness, helplessness or maybe That where all the hope comes from. But you cannot end yourself, so you cannot end the hope. You are the wishlessness that will always create another wish and you are helpless. By you trying to end the wish, you wish for the end of the wish. That makes you a wisher – wishing something – a witch doctor. Then you ask – In which way can I end myself? Then you become a witch.

Then there are others – so-called – they claim that they made it. Then I always ask – How can someone call off the search? Who is the one who calls off the search? And who did it? Bullshit! From a seeker to a finder, who says this bullshit? Where does it come from? From a phantom, who claims that he gained something, he reached some point, he made it. So, it needs someone who landed somewhere. Even by saying that there's nowhere to land, he landed on the 'no landing'. Even the 'no landing' is one landing too many. Strange!

But ignorance is unbelievable. It has infinite traps. And being a guru and having made it and having realized the truth, is one of the biggest traps. So, even *gurus* are living in a trap. What to do? Especially the big ones – the bigger me's. Especially the ones with power – they are in the power trap – *siddhi* trap. So many traps!

I would make much more money and more people would come,

if I would not destroy all of that. If I would not say all of this. Sometimes Karl would say that before he comes – maybe today I say something nice that makes people comfortable, make life a bit more easy. But when I sit here... [Laughing] It becomes a joke, all my plans.

There is one absolute thing – I would kill myself right away before I bullshit myself. And I would lose all the people who came or will come just if I had to say because I have to please someone. I would just turn away and kill myself. So, fuck you all – in that sense.

Q [Another visitor]: So, you can't bullshit yourself anymore, somehow?

K: I do. By not trying to bullshit myself, I bullshit myself. Even by claiming that I do not bullshit myself, I bullshit myself.

Q: But it's a happening...

K: There's just a helplessness running me. It's like I cannot decide to wake up in the morning. But maybe I start to talk nicer. [Laughter]

Q [Another visitor]: Try now...

K: I do sometimes – surprisingly. Sometimes I say nice things and I see that people are enjoying. Then one minute later, I take it away. I do it, but I cannot stay in it. Sometimes it happens, but then comes the other side and destroys it right away.

Q: So, one is better than the other?

K: All of that is bullshit. But it has to be balanced.

Q [Another visitor]: The bottom-line is as you say everything is a misunderstanding, you have to destroy it...

K: I do it all the time.

Q: So, that's a contradiction...

K: I'm a paradox myself. But that's called Ramana's good company

– being the paradox and destroying what you just said. Leaving nothing, giving nothing, taking nothing. The contradiction has to be there. You have to contradict whatever you say – instantly and there are only a few, Nisargadatta [Maharaj] and Ranjit [Maharaj] who did it.

For many teachers, you can repeat what they say. They don't contradict, they are very clear. They don't contradict themselves and you can live with that. That I really hate – that it really works! It makes you more happy, more content, more comfortable and that for me is the biggest bullshit – whatever has a result.

Q [Another visitor]: There are some things you say that you cannot contradict...

K: Be-what-you-cannot-not-be, I can contradict. It's very easy to contradict. Who said it and who wants to hear it? One is too many and no-one is too much. It's always possible.

I always enjoy when people try to repeat what I have said. Some clever ones say – You may have said – as I understood you. Even I cannot repeat what I say. Crazy! But there are books you can read. [Laughter] Books don't work – nor do no-books.

Q [Another visitor]: It's amazing, just lying here with closed eyes, listening to you, things just passing through...

K: Now you become one of these lying bastards here. [Laughter] Very soon all will just lie here in front of me and I'll just talk to corpses. [Laughter] They all let it go through.

February 12, 2012. Morning Talk.
Thailand

I Am That – What is stupidity itself

Q: I'm still looking for a result...

K: That makes you retired and I promise that you wouldn't find one. None of this what you can say is yours – all stolen, all second hand, no question which is yours.

Q: There's a tendency to find the original question...

K: If you stay in That, after a while the questioner will be gone. If you really go for the original question which would be yours, you could not find one and in not finding the question, you would be gone. Martin could not exist in That. The questioner can only exist in the imaginary – 'my question', but it's all stolen, there's no 'your' question – all second hand. So, try harder.

Q [Another visitor]: So what about giving up trying?

K: Then there's still one who gave up trying and he's very proud because he's not trying but the other ones are still trying. So, what to do with it?

Q: No way out...

K: So, now we go to the next questioner. [Laughter]

Q [Another visitor]: I wanted to ask about psychological imprint. Is it that memory created consciousness and gets identified with a perception?

K: No. Perception cannot be identified. It needs an 'I' to be identified, but perception has no 'I'. In perception there's an 'I' that gets identified and that wants to get dis-identified. It's a game of 'I'. Only the 'I' gets identified, perception cannot get identified. Perception is like a canvas which cannot get identified with anything. The 'I', the lover, the first, the primal – that can fall in love. Perception cannot fall in love.

Q: Consciousness can?

K: Consciousness can. That's already the 'I' – the awareness 'I' where the consciousness starts with a lover. Then falling in love happens and by falling in love, the identification starts.

Q: So, once consciousness gets identified, is it always identified or is it possible to get dis-identified?

K: After a while it's not so comfortable anymore, so it tries to dis-identify with it.

Q: But is it possible?

K: Yeah, for some it happens. The phantom 'I' gets identified and then by whatever it becomes a seeker, and out of seeking, trying to understand, it becomes dis-identified with a non-identified 'I'. Then they call it the 'choiceless awareness I' – the non-identified 'I' – the masters talk from there. A non-identified 'I' talks to an identified 'I'.

The impersonal consciousness talks to a personal consciousness. The personal consciousness is identified consciousness and impersonal is dis-identified. The cosmic consciousness talks to the individual consciousness.

Q: A couple of weeks back I was reminded of an incident from the past. Once there was a person who approached me when I was drunk and I could unconsciously recognize a danger. But I have no idea what this person wanted from me...

K: Maybe out of the past life there was a same circumstance.

Q: Then comes the question of reincarnation...

K: Can happen.

Q: What is it?

K: It's like information from past is remembered by consciousness and it's reacting out of the memory.

Q: But consciousness is reacting to consciousness?

K: Consciousness has all the memories of all what is possible. You are like a cluster of all the information before which comes from whatever ancestors. It's a cluster. Maybe one of your ancestors had a similar circumstance and one of your cell's energy reacted to it because there was a memory. All this is energetic conditioning from whatever past. So, it's not you reacting, maybe it's your grand, grand, grandma had a similar experience with a similar guy. Who knows?

Q: Sometimes a person comes and even if maybe he's lovely, it feels like someone is trying to swallow you...

K: Maybe in that circumstance you were killed by someone or maybe he stole your banana.

Q: So, what is it, that is afraid?

K: Maybe after that event, there was a very intense discomfort that happened – a circumstance that you really don't like. You never know why you like somebody and why not. You never know why things happen.

Q: But these reactions come from consciousness?

K: They come from consciousness. You can call it sub-consciousness, but it's consciousness – then you're not conscious where it comes from. If you find a circumstance from childhood, of why your reaction happened, then it becomes conscious. But if you cannot find the circumstance, it stays in sub-conscious and then you forget it. When you find why you do it, you make it a story again. And because you make it a story, you remember. I think giving attention to it is already too much.

Q: I know, but it doesn't go away...

K: Why should it go away? It will go away when the body goes. It's early enough. Or maybe you go to a psychoanalyst for years and lay down on the couch to really find out and then maybe you get so bored, that you drop it out of boredom, but not by solving something. [Laughter] All the psychotherapists live from that. The bloody family constipation [mocking family constellation therapy] worldwide is living by that. Why not?

Q: So, this information will be there?

K: It will always be there. You are like a cluster of information from your past. The totality made this form, which is a cluster from all the forms from the past, and now this information reacts as it reacts.

Q: But is it possible to get out of this cluster of information?

K: No! Why should you?

Q: It might happen...

K: And what would be the advantage?

Q: No advantage, it's just a matter of fact.

K: Just as it got identified, it may get dis-identified. Sooner or later you drop this body anyway. If maybe today or when this [body] goes to the grave. Does it matter when it goes? It will be gone one day. The only thing that counts is that it will be gone. So, it's not even there now. It doesn't exist now because it will be gone one day, and whatever will be gone one day is not real. So, it's an imaginary, phenomenal what? Temporary [blowing in the wind] – body experience. It comes with the body and it will be gone with the body.

All of that will be gone with the body and in one instant, it was never ever there and you still will be what-you-are.

Q: So, the only thing that's left is just go through it?

K: Just enjoy the ride. There was a beginning of this ride with this body and there will be an end of this ride with this body. It's like a movie, which has a beginning and has an end. But the perception-you-are was there before the movie started and will be there after the movie ended and even now it's there. So, nothing will happen.

Nothing happened in the beginning and nothing will happen at the end, as nothing is happening now. So, it will all be gone in the past again, in darkness of whatever was before. So, why worry about what is already gone? Part of it is even enlightenment experiences, or awakenings. All of that is part of the story – it will be gone one day. So what to do with it? Enjoy it as long as it lasts and as long as there's a body, there will be a memory of it, but when the body is gone, all the memories sink back to darkness of past, it's not available. Maybe with the next body there's an echo from the past and then you experience something again and you ask – where did it come from? There was something.

It's like a *deja vu* again. I remember, but I don't know what. You will ask yourself again – what was it? Again and again. Out of love for yourself, this loving business here [pointing to the body], he wants to know what happened with his beloved. He wants to make a diary out of it, writing it down. The memories and the precious insights and discoveries. You are like a discovery channel.

Q: In the manifestation, there's no way out of the mind?

K: How can the mind leave the mind? It's a joke. The mind wants to leave the mind.

Q: Is awareness also mind – the 'I' thought?

K: It's all mind. We already talked about it. With awareness separation starts, so the mind starts – two. So, where there is consciousness, there's two and all of that is mind, so never mind. Wherever you can land, is in mind – mind lands in mind and only mind gets identified with mind. It's a different kind of mind and only mind minds the mind. And that will never stop. So, it's a monkey mind. What to do?

Worry and be happy! The worries come by themselves because the mind will mind the mind – if you like it or not. There may be a temporary pause in it – like a peace of mind. But what can be in peace, can be in war again. There's a temporary pause and then it starts fucking again.

Q: There was a moment when I was going through a difficult time and then there was an experience of awareness in background somewhere. I felt like it did not matter...

K: There's always an uninterrupted carelessness, being untouched, unchangeable. You can call it something that cannot be changed by something else.

Q: It seems there was a knowledge that it will come and it will go...

K: I would call it the absence and the presence. The absence cannot be touched by the presence. As if everything around is a fleeting shadow and what one-is, is – untouched by it. There's no danger in it.

Q: So, being aware is just an escape?

K: You don't have to be aware – to be aware. It's like a paradox. You don't have to be aware to be that what is the awareness. It's naturally there. Without that awareness, there's nothing that can happen. Then every night there's absence of awareness or awakeness, and still you are – what-you-are. So, what happens? Nothing happens.

Q: Yesterday we were talking about the primal notion, the awareness, the 'I' is already discomfort and I remember it's true. I had an operation few months ago and they put me on anaesthesia. When I came out of it, my reaction was – shit I woke up!

K: Yeah. I always tell the story of my mother who came out of coma. The first word pronounced was – shit! It's natural. If you pronounce the first word – shit – back in business.

Q: Yeah. I thought I can have another day of absence...

K: Every night you go to the absolute absence and then – shit! Out of the blue, waking up happens. Then the business starts again. Every morning this is experience of helplessness. It's impossible not to wake up and when you're awake, it's too late. Then you have to wait until it goes by itself. So, you work your ass off just for the next sleep – that you can go back to the comfort zone.

Some don't want to wake up, they drink and drink. It's called the 'coma drinking'. They try to stay permanently in the state of absence. Some work their ass off, some run a marathon – just to go to the absence, the dead point. Meditating! All of that is for trying to be absent, because the presence is too much. Every one is fed up – from the beginning. The baby cries from the moment it's there, and then it gets something to be quiet.

Q: Sometimes there's a void, a feeling of complete emptiness. It's like there's nothing to cling on to. Once I had a panic attack with this sense of emptiness. It seems contradictory. Why does that happen?

K: That's what you are longing for – that's grace but when that happens, you piss in your trousers.

Q: Why?

K: Because you cannot exist in there. It's the most dangerous absence. The 'me' cannot exist in the absence of the second. It's impossible. Even Jesus went into the desert for forty days. He went not to the desert but to the void and then the mind came back, the devil tempting him. But he just remained in the void and by remaining in the void for whatever time, the 'me' dissolved. That was his preparation for being crucified.

All the stories of passion of Christ and crucifixion is not an outside story. It's an inside way of reaching that helplessness and helplessness is the symbol of the cross – being crucified. That you cannot absolutely move any more. Being totally fixed on what-you-are. It's not a story of a drama or something. It's like you being crucified. This is like you are being crucified more and more so that the helplessness takes over – that's grace.

The Self becomes more and more – that what is unmovable. Crucifying itself in the helplessness, that it cannot do anything. You will be crucified on what-you-are. In the horizontal time, in the vertical spirit and the Heart in center – you are that and you will be crucified. Part of the preparation for this crucifixion is that the void becomes more and more. The senselessness of your surroundings becomes more and more. Nothing makes you happy anymore, everything becomes empty. The relation-shit(ship) – all of that becomes like shit.

Nothing gives you satisfaction. All is empty. No drinking, no friends, no family, no work. All of that becomes [blowing in the wind] – empty! Like a void. No hope anymore in anything. No comfort you can find in any little thing. Before you were in the *ashram* and you were so happy with the energy and the *shakti* bullshit. Now it's so empty. Even this light bullshit, the *kundalini* – who bloody needs it? All of that becomes completely empty and that's called grace.

Q [Another visitor]: And then?

K: Nothing then. You're just crucified to what-you-are – that's all. You get pierced by the spear of destiny. Your destiny is that you have to face yourself infinitely. There's no 'then'. There will always be Zen and Zen and Zen – the infinite Zen – the hope that there will be an end – drops, but there's no end to it. So, in the end, there's no end. There's no 'then'. You still hope for something. That you will get some prize. There's no prize to get. You want a gold medal like you went through all of that and now you want something out of it – pay day. There's no pay day. This last hope will drop – judgment day.

You will be judged and if there's a little Michael left, he will be demolished. The absolute payment is like being what-you-cannot-not-be, there's a fulfillment beyond imagination, which was always there, never needed any comfort in any sense. No sense can give you any comfort. That's the pay day – that there's no comfort for you and that's quite peaceful. That's the peace itself, that there is no comfort for you. It's not a peace you can find, that comes over you and dissolves you and eats you up. No! The peace was always there. So, peace-off!

Q [Another visitor]: Although sometimes I have moments of despair, but I think it's the mind that gets frustrated...

K: The little fisherman inside still wants a fish to fish and it still hopes that there will be a fish sooner or later that satisfies you. You're still fishing. Then the fishing starts again. You spin a web where you can catch something, until the energy is gone and it collapses again. Then you're back to the absence, but then you try again. The fishing will never stop.

But maybe the expectation drops – more and more. The expectation that by catching something, there will really be something to catch. You're fishing something but there's nothing to catch. But still you have to fish.

Q: I guess this is the mechanism of survival...

K: You have to get up in the morning, go to the toilet, eat your breakfast and the next and the next. It's like you do your job but you don't expect that one of that makes you happy. It's just an automatic fulfillment of the job that has to be done. It's an automatic doing – things happen by themselves. But not out of one expecting to get happy out of it. [Mocking] Today I had the biggest breakfast of my life and I will be happy ever after. [Laughter]

No! You just have the bloody breakfast. The next sip of coffee. That's the nature of the next sip of coffee. The thirst comes back again, so there's the next, the next and the next – never ending.

Q: But something gets weaker, relaxed?

K: But that what can get weaker, can get strong again, I tell you. Again and again. It's like it's hiding in the corner and suddenly it wakes up again. [Mocking] Hey! I'm still here baby! You thought I was gone? Ha, ha, ha.

Q: As you said the other day we think some situations in life are finished. But it finishes when it finishes...

K: And then comes something else.

Q: However it seems some energy is left out...

K: And then comes another aspect of life that wants to be left out. Don't think that you will be clean enough that there's no tendency left. This body will always have a tendency until it goes to the grave.

Q: It's so stupid to go through the same thing again and again...

K: But you are stupid that you're alive! To exist already is stupid. To wake up is dumb – the 'I'. To live – I Amness – is dumber. To have a body, is dumbest. Dumb, dumber, dumbest – that's the way you live right now. What to do? If it already starts dumb and on top of it comes dumber and then comes the dumbest – the identification with this one. What to do? And you cannot avoid to be dumb.

But it's already okay. The dumb [lifting the thumb] means okay, but this [raising the middle finger] means fuck you all – having a body. You are the joker. You are fooling yourself with that one first [lifting his thumb], then that one [raising the index finger] and then with this one [raising the middle finger].

You are realizing yourself as a fool and you're always fooling yourself. You are the absolute fool, fooling only yourself – by imagining to have awareness, being conscious and then having a body. It's fooling yourself. But by trying not to fool yourself, you become the biggest fool. Fooling is natural, you lie to yourself. Your real-lie-zation comes with a real-lie-zer. That's the biggest lie – the first liar! The creator lie. Then creating lying and what can be lied. The real-lie-zation of what-you-are – the Reality! Reality lying to Reality by real-lie-zation. It's a tell-lie-vision. Look, this is all a soap opera of the Self.

That's why when Ramana or Nisargadatta say you have to realize yourself, they're pointing to your nature which you can call Reality or Self – Parabrahma – call it whatever. You cannot stop realizing yourself. You have to realize yourself – in whatever way. Sometimes it's more or less comfort or discomfort. Whatever you call it, this all is what-you-are and you are That!

When Nisargadatta says – I Am That – means I am realizing That what is realizing itself as 'I Am That' and you cannot stop that. There will always be a – then – the next and the next and the next. After this body tra...la...la, there will be something else. In this case your neighbor will still be alive, because your neighbor is still your realization. The sun, the universe, none of that will go if this body is gone. Your bloody nature will realize itself as the next moment. No way out!

And then solving some little problems of body – God oh God! Having some senseless moments or the touching of the void and a little despair. All of that has to be experienced. All of that is part of your realization. In all ways! In the most profound and the most bullshit.

Q [Another visitor]: So, I Am That is I am realizing myself as whatever. I always thought it was the opposite...

K: No, no. I Am That means I Am That – not naming it, but still I Am – That. Because he is the 'I', he is the 'I Am' and he is 'That' what is the eye. You are That what is the 'I', you are the 'I Am' and you are That what is the universe and I Am That. As reality is not different from realization, the nature of realization is reality. The nature of ignorance is knowledge. There is only knowledge experiencing itself in ignorance, but it doesn't get ignorant by that. So, even the nature of ignorance is knowledge.

There is only light or knowledge – call it whatever. There is no second. That's why it's *Advaita* – no two. So, ignorance is not different from knowledge because the nature of ignorance is knowledge. I Am That – what is ignorance, I Am That – what is stupidity. I Am That – what is the asshole. But can I smell myself? No! Whatever I smell is just – I don't know what it is...

Q [Another visitor]: Someone told me that you also realize that you are everything...

K: No way out. It's quite a shock isn't it? When the hope drops that there's a way out. When you are everything, there's no way out. So, first it's quite a shock, but then you get used to it – don't worry. [Laughter] Because if there's no way out, sooner or later you get used to it. What to do? You get used to everything. You already got used to having a body, that's itself quite a shock – to be born.

The 'being born' shock is much bigger. Then the shock that you cannot get out of it, goes away because that understanding drops sooner or later. It came and it will be gone. It's still part of a relative realization that you are everything. It's part of ignorance – will always change. Then some other understanding comes but your nature will still be what-it-is.

Q [Another visitor]: Prior to the realization – 'I Am That'...

K: When there's absence, you are the absence and that's prior to the presence. When you are presence, you are the presence. You are That what is the absence when there's absence. You are the presence when there's presence. When there's neither absence or presence, you are That what is neither absence or presence. You are That what is – that-what-is – whatever it is. There's nothing other than you.

Q: And that's being what-I-cannot-not-be?

K: That you cannot not be!

Q: In the absence and the presence?

K: You are the absence in the absence and you are the presence in the presence. But there's no one in the absence and no one in the presence.

Q: Am I aware in presence?

K: Who is awareness?

Q: Me! [Laughter]

K: [Mocking] So, we all are not awareness because 'you' are awareness. From now onwards awareness will be called Michael – the arch angel – the awareness angel. [Laughter]

Whatever you identify yourself with is bullshit. Identification means two – one who identifies himself with something else. So, the moment you say – I Am Awareness – it's already two awarenesses. There's the 'I' and there's the awareness. Then you have to fish and fight for that reference point. You have to pronounce it and whatever you can pronounce – is pronounced shit or pro-found shit – because whatever can be found is shit!

No! What-you-cannot-not-be is, every night in deep-deep sleep: you exist – as what-you-are in the absence.

Q: Is there awareness in deep-deep sleep?

K: Doesn't matter. Who needs awareness to exist? Say it!

Q: Me! [Laughter]

K: Yeah. [Laughing] So, Master phantom needs awareness to exist. What kind of reality would it be that needs awareness to exist?

Q: It would be a fucking limited one...

K: It's a fucking phantom, yes. Then the fucking phantom called the mind that minds around – all day long. That's called mind-fucking mind and then the mind-fucking mind pronounces that – I Am the awareness! What the fuck does this mind think he is?

Q: A 'someone'...

K: Yeah... and then that someone even claims to be awareness. Then he even claims that I Am choiceless awareness – me! Then tells others that you are choiceless awareness. [Mocking] You have to realize that you are only the choiceless awareness. [Laughter]

Q: Been there done that...

K: Many times! That's called master-bation – one jerk telling another jerk the right way of how to jerk-off – the master jerk! [Mocking] This is your true nature, being identified with your body is not your true nature. That's wrong, but if you are identified with awareness, then you are in your true nature. Abide in it – take a bite in it. [Laughter]

Q [Laughing]: So what to do? After being there, I went back to washing dishes...

K: The next sip of coffee is washing dishes. So what?

Q: Profound shit...

K: Whatever you can find is shit. It's very profound, then the next shit happens and the next shit. So what? In the relative world everything is shit and in the non-relative, everything is shit. The time is shit, the no-time is shit and even where the time and no-time starts – is shit. Even the beyond is shit because you cannot stay in the beyond. If that would be your nature, why do you drop out of it again? Then you are back here. Absence is shit, presence is shit.

That's why I like shit so much because there's nothing else that I can like. I love it! No way out! The way out is shit, the no way out is shit. No peace to find. The peace you find is a peace of shit.

Q: No peace to lose...

K: Waste the time you don't have. That's the famous Australian saying – been there done that – what next? That's why I can talk infinitely because there's nothing that comes out of it. No effort – shit happens by itself.

Q [Another visitor]: Just as you say shit, shit, shit, I can say pudding, pudding, pudding or love, love, love. Everyone has their own ideas...

K: If you say love, love, love then maybe you give attention to it. The last attention you give to – is shit. You are conditioned that shit is lowest because it comes out of your ass. You cannot sell your shit, that's why it's called shit. You can sell love again to others, but no one wants shit from you. That's why shit is the best because not even you want it and no one else wants to buy it from you. That's why you call it shit. Otherwise if you call it pudding, maybe someone likes pudding. [Laughter]

Q [Another visitor]: But people like having a good shit... [Laughter]

K: [Mocking] That's the wisdom from Down Under. The kangaroo wisdom – when I 'can', I'm released.

You are right, because it's the lowest, you don't pick it up. The possibility that you leave it as it is – is higher than that you pick it up and it comes easy. As she said when she woke up from anaesthesia the first word that comes naturally is – shit. So, it all starts as shit, in a way and when you eat, you know it's shit. The future of whatever you eat, is shit. The future of whatever you see, will be gone, so it's shit. The future of your every experience will be – shit.

The most precious sunset – shit. The most precious orgasm – shit. Sooner or later, it's over – even the longest one. Even the longest period of enlightenment. Because enlightenment came, it will be gone one day, so it's shit. The awakening that happened, will be gone one day, so it's shit. How can reality come and go? In what? So, whatever comes and goes, is shit. I like it. [Laughter]

When everything is shit, there's suddenly a carelessness. Because whatever-is and is-not is shit, it's like peace. It's a peace of shit.

Q [Another visitor]: I have a question about tendencies...

K: Dentistry? You are here for a root treatment. [Laughter] If you don't have a tooth anymore, it can't hurt anymore. The tooth maybe there but after root treatment, there's no one who's experiencing the tooth. So, there's no connection between you and the tooth. That's called a root treatment. Perception was never connected to the tooth.

So, what was your question? [Laughter]

Q: When tendencies arise, you can perform an action…

K: Any tendency comes from a root tendency that you want to be happy. The first root thought 'I' is like, I want to know or I want to be happy. That's the root tendency. All that you can talk about are like variations of trying to be happy. Trying to get out of the discomfort of existence. The tendency of comfort, the tendency of peace, all that you can do, the outcome will be peace.

So, every wish is wishing for wishlessness – the end of the wish. You wish the end of the wish, but your trying to end the wish keeps the wish alive. So, the tendency to end the tendency, keeps the tendency alive. It's a trap. The more you want to end it, you feed it. It's counter productive. As much as you know yourself, you become more ignorant, because absolute not knowing yourself is the nature of knowledge.

Knowledge doesn't need to know knowledge. It is knowledge. There's no knower or no-knower who can never know that which is knowledge. Whatever the knower – which already is an ignorance – can know, is an ignorant knowledge. It's a relative knowledge and the intention is always to make the relative knowledge into absolute knowledge. But it will never happen.

So, out of relative peace or knowledge, it will never become the absolute peace or knowledge, but this tendency, you cannot stop. No way of stopping it. Because consciousness cannot stop trying to know consciousness, the inquiry will never stop. The love of consciousness for itself, cannot be stopped. The lover loving the beloved, which is consciousness, is a way of realization. It will never stop.

So, the tendency is always love. And out of love, it wants to know itself. But because it wants to know itself, it doesn't know itself, but it's still consciousness. So, nothing happens. So, inspite of the tendency that you have to know yourself, you have to be what-you-are. That there can be one doubting himself, inquiring into himself, that there can be consciousness at all, there has to be That what is consciousness – neither knowing nor not knowing itself. It has to be there so that there can be a one who knows or doesn't know – for doubting or not doubting, that doubtlessness of existence has to-be.

Ramakrishna Parahamsa's basic teaching was that I can doubt myself. But prior to the doubter – that I experience myself as a doubter doubting myself – the doubtlessness of the existence has to be there. Without the doubtlessness of the existence, there is no possibility of the presence of a doubter, doubting to exist or not to exist. That's all.

The doubtlessness is the absolute omnipresence, which is never-never – has to-be before even the imaginary doubter can doubt or not doubt. Even the possibility of one who could or could-not can only be there because the doubtlessness of what-is – has to-be. Prior beyond of all presences and absences – That doubtless is. That there can be a presence or absence at all – That has to-be – and That is what-you-are, That you cannot-not-be, and That is realizing itself as all that whatever doubting or not doubting.

So, we have to look here. That this table can be here, that we can talk, even talking or not talking, doubting – whatever can be – without that evident doubtlessness of whatever you call it, has to be. That unpronounceable – whatever it is has to be there, that it can pronounce itself as all of that that is here. That there can be pronouncer pronouncing whatever can be pronounced, the thinker thinking whatever can be thought, there has to be that nature of whatever you call it.

And that you are in deep-deep sleep, as you are here-now – That

– what never comes, never goes, which is in coming not coming and in going not going. That coming can be there, what-you-are, has to be. That going can be, you have to be there. So, before the coming, during and after the going – you are That. Then comes the next coming and the next going.

I'm just pointing to That more than open secret – That there is no secret. That there can only be a secret or an idea about a secret, That has to be and to be That what-you-cannot-not-be is beyond all the ideas of fulfillment and peace and anything. It's all beyond all imaginary senses and sensational experiences. All of that compared to what-you-are, is a piece of shit.

Q: As long as form is present, this understanding will just be mental?

K: It will always be mental. Every understanding is mental. That what-you-are, never needs to understand anything to be what-it-is. Every fucking understanding, every realization is mental.

Q: That's what I meant when I said the other day, realization is in the mind...

K: No. You realize yourself in the mind, but you are not the mind and mind is simply two. You can only realize yourself as two – that's mind. Mind means two, that's time, that's two, but there's no other way. You can only realize yourself as a creator which is different from the creation or the seer which is different from what is seen. There is no other way.

You can only realize yourself as an owner, owning what can be owned. All of that is the way you realize yourself – in whatever way. But by all of that, you cannot know yourself – in any relative sense.

Q: That's why you say that there's no truth...

K: The truth that has to be true, cannot be true, because it's a depending truth. The truth which depends on truth, cannot be true. The nature of peace doesn't need any peace to be peace and the truth that needs to be true, cannot be true. Freedom that needs to be free, is not freedom. You will never be free from yourself. So, freedom doesn't know any freedom and freedom is what-is because there's a freedom from a second. But there's no possible way that the freedom can be free. From what? How can you be free? From what? You are That. How can you be free from That?

Freedom is just a pointer that there's no second, that you can be bound to. You cannot be connected to someone or anything because there's no two. That's the freedom of two. But you cannot be free 'from' anything because you are whatever-is and is-not. How can you be free from yourself? Freedom doesn't need any freedom, but 'me' always wants to be free.

Q: So you can't even say that you are zero?

K: You are the zero of the zero. The zero that doesn't know any zero. That what knows zero is already one too many. So, you are the zero-zero which is also the number for toilet – call it shit. If you see it as zero (0) it is the awareness, if you turn it around, from the side-view it becomes one (1) and if you bend it it becomes eight (8), the infinite. The same zero shows itself as zero (0), the one (1) and the eight (8). That's why *Shiva*'s number is 108. One(1) is the awareness, zero(0) is the void and eight(8) is the infinite incarnation of infinite drama of infinite manifestation. I like the Indians. The zero was invented in India.

Q: That's why later could invent computers...

K: Imagine the bits and bytes without zero. No apple! Maybe it would not have been so bad. [Laughter] Pod in Germany means toilet – I-pod. The next one will be I-shit! This is called the Stockholm syndrome. Everyone is kidnapped by Apple and now they are in love with the kidnapper. Now they even defend it. I can't do anything with it, but I love it. [Laughter] It tells me what to do, it's the most fascistic machine on earth – but I love it. [Mocking] At least it looks good, at least you look good with it.

Q: That's real love!

K: Yeah. It's like a wife you cannot fuck, but you love her anyway – that's true love. [Laughter] If you can do something with your wife, it's not true love. True love is just there not because of what she can do or not do, just because she's there – platonic – I-platonic.

Q [Another visitor]: That which is never-never, it never shows?

K: Even to say that it never shows is too much. You can never experience it as it-is. The nature, you cannot experience but still it shows itself in every possible way. The nature can never be known. Whatever can be known are reflections, call it whatever. It's a realization you can experience, but not Reality. Reality will never experience Reality in its nature. It can realize itself in all possible way, but not as it-is.

You have to be what-you-are without knowing what-it-is. But the moment you know it, you know yourself as shit. Whenever you know anything, instantly the knower already is shit – it's relative. Any knower, knowing or not knowing is already relative. Whatever the knower knows, is relative knowing something – relative, objective knowledge. It's not what's the nature because in nature there's no two and for any knowing it needs two. Impossible!

So, you have to stay as a mystery for yourself. That's why they call it absolute absence of any idea or no-idea of what-you-are and what-you-are-not. All the ideas come from the first root thought 'I'. Then come all the ideas of what-you-are and what-you-are-not. Then comes identification and non-identification, doership and non-doership.

But inspite of the presence of the 'I' thought, you are That what is in the presence and in the absence – That what-you-are. But you will never know That, in any relative sense. Absolutely you know it by being it, what-you-cannot-not-be. That's Absolute knowledge. That you know by heart, not by mind.

[A visitor sneezes]

Drop dead you beast! [Laughter] I mean the virus. [Laughter] Everyone says bless you. Ha, ha, ha! They just mean shut up.

Q [Another visitor]: When you talk about the Absolute being as-it-is, unknowable...

K: That's why it's called the Absolute – no two.

Q: But the realization must continue anyway. So what you are describing is – that all the people here are dream objects and also the Absolute. So, what you are saying is the sense of being an Absolute takes precedence over the sense of being a phantom. For me there's a contradiction between when you say hope is what keeps us alive...

K: What is meant by your head is in tiger's mouth is, that what sits here will be dead sooner or later. It is already in the tiger's mouth and you still will be what-you-are. Everyone takes it personal and thinks that I'm closer to my bloody enlightenment or awakening. No! Your destiny is that this body-mind organism is *kaput* [German for broken] one day. You are already in the tiger's mouth and [snaps his fingers] last moment happens – and then comes something else.

That's the tiger's mouth. So, your destiny is fixed. You are already dead. [Mocking] It's not like as if I am a seeker now and my head is already in the tiger's mouth and I am in the right direction and grace takes me over and it will take me to the beyond. NO! Your bloody destiny is already fixed. You are already dead. [Laughter] What else can it mean?

It is anyway a paper tiger. Whatever can die is not dying because it was never alive. So, what's the problem?

Q [Another visitor]: You're taking the last hope away!

K: That's what all Masters point to. They point to the fact that you are already dead. This vessel is already gone. It doesn't matter how empty it is or how much it knows, it will be gone one day. So, it's already dead. It doesn't exist and you always put all your interest in bullshit – in a piece of shit which is already gone, especially your head. There was never any truth in it.

But everyone takes it fucking personal and thinks that my head is already in tiger's mouth and there's a process that sooner or later it will be gone. No, the process is this [body] is processed already by the worms eating it up or by the fire licking it to the ashes. I'm talking to ashes here – ashes to ashes.

Q [Another visitor]: So, when you say be-what-you-cannot-not-be...

K: That is not a body, that is not an idea, that is not what can be in the tiger's mouth.

Q: That's what we already are...

K: Yeah. So, why are you talking about the tiger's mouth and a process?

Q: I just try to describe the process that seems to be double bound...

K: No. You take it as double bound. Everyone took it as double bound that when Ramana told that you have to realize yourself, you take it personal that you have to realize 'your' true nature. It's bullshit. You will never realize your true nature. You are already your nature which is realizing itself. That was the pointer. He was not talking to 'someone' who has to realize himself. He was never talking to a person.

Q: So you say, nothing-is, nothing-is, nothing-is...

K: I don't even say nothing-is. [Laughter] Now you put your money on nothing. It's a lame horse – the nothing is a lame horse and everything is a lame horse. Already dead horses, it's a dead race. Whatever you put your money on, is dead. It's all a cemetery of life. A tombstone can infinitely be in the tiger's mouth, but it will still be a tombstone.

Q: So, when you describe the loss of interest...

K: I just describe a movie. There's nothing in it for anybody.

Q: So, you're saying that in the movie it can happen that the interest moves from the relative to the Absolute...

K: I call it the passion of Christ and Christ is already the Buddha-nature which has to experience itself in all possible ways. That's one possible way of experiencing yourself – that's all. No one ever attained himself by any process. That's why it's a passion of Christ. Christ is a pointer to your Buddha-nature, your Christ-nature. It's a synonym.

It's all a passion of Christ – the love story of yourself which has infinite different ways of loving and having a story. All this Romeo and Juliet blah, blah, blah. It's a never ending story – there's no end to it. It's an infinite love story with yourself. [Mocking] Tiger's mouth. [Laughing]

It's like existence takes this [body] as a vibrator and vibrates a little bit – that's all. As if it could be more orgasmic then it already is. I know that's impossible. I talk to that-what-you-are and the one who hears it takes it personally – yes me, too! [Mocking] Am I already in the tiger's mouth? Am I processing? Am I already ripening? Am I the apple that will fall sooner or later anyway? All these images – when the apple is ripe, the right farmer will come and pick it and stew it slowly – that it could be eaten by life.

Actually who wants to be in tiger's mouth? It stinks – I tell you. [Laughter] It never brushes it's teeth – yuck! Is that a preparation for the corpse? Being in the tiger's mouth. [Laughter]

Q [Another visitor]: When you say this, the romance goes away so quickly...

K: I'm the most romantic on earth I tell you. [Laughter] No one believes me. I'm in an absolute love-affair with myself. There's no discrimination on how to fuck myself. You have an idea of romance – how it has to be, how tender. The romance with yourself is not always tender. Sometimes you fuck yourself really hard and sometimes very soft. But always differently, and you are always fucked by yourself – if you like it or not, and you cannot decide how you fuck yourself next time. [Laughter]

And you are the cruelest lover that you can imagine to yourself. You are cruelest with yourself. Absolute carelessness running and fucking around with itself. As you absolutely know inside that nothing can happen. It's like the consciousness inside saying – whatever I can do, I will do. Look at what is happening in this world. All these wars and earthquakes, people dying and family dramas. The most dangerous place is a family. There are more killings in a family than anywhere else.

Q [Another visitor]: So all what you described, is it a love-affair?

K: Of course! This is all created by energy fucking energy, life fucking life. The whole universe is a result of love.

Q: What you just described seemed it's a hell...

K: It's a hell of a love. [Laughter] Love is hell because in love you experience yourself as different from the beloved and that's the nature of hell. So, fucking can only happen in hell. In your nature, you cannot fuck yourself because there are no two. So, you have to imagine yourself in an imaginary fucking place – which is called the universe where you play your little drama with yourself. This is your stage and you always play Romeo and Juliet – fucking.

And then you want to be the tiger's mouth because you are fed up with your beloved – No I don't want to fuck anymore. [Laughter] I keep quiet, I don't vibrate anymore, I don't cum anymore – not me. [Laughter] The whole fucking milky way came from that – God cuming. It's crazy!

Q: Totally...

K: You are crazy – I tell you. Then you always want to analyze in what kind of process you are now and what will happen next and what happened in the past and all the Masters and how much help do I need and when will it end. Maybe I don't have enough time left. Maybe I should fuck more or maybe not fucking is better. Maybe fucking is against the inner direction. [Laughter] It's called the inner erection. I should take care about my inner self and not fuck the outer self too much. [Laughter] So, many ideas! The kamasutra – inner cuming and the outer cuming. What an outcome! It's crazy!

Q [Another visitor jokingly]: At least there's an in-cum...

K: There's an in-cum with your out-cum. You are your own pimp and your own whore – you know that.

Q [Another visitor]: In the morning you said that resistance makes us tired. So, how would it be without resistance?

K: You would be tired too. [Laughter]

Q: And how do I create resistance?

K: Because you fuck yourself or you don't want to fuck – that makes you tired. So, fucking makes you tired and not fucking makes you tired. You get tired anyway. So, don't worry. [Laughter]

Q: But what do you mean by resistance? I want it to be clear...

K: Because you want to be clear, you resist. Because you want to understand, you resist understanding. Because you want to have it, it doesn't happen. By trying to get it, you don't get it. By wanting to be what-you-are, you are something other than what-you-are.

Q: But I can't stop the wanting...

K: I didn't say that you can stop the wanting.

Q: So, it's something totally natural...

K: Yeah. I didn't say it's not natural for you. Resistance is the nature of the mind. Without resistance, there would be no mind. So, mind has to resist. Then it gets tired and only when mind gets tired, sleep happens. Then every morning the mind has rested again and it's full of power and then it starts resisting again.

Q: It's strange when I follow what you are saying without my mind, then it stops the worrying. If I don't do that, then the worrying is stronger...

K: Worry gets stronger if you don't follow me. If you follow me, I lead you to a place where you cannot breath.

Q: Then there comes a point where you completely drop...

K: Yeah. You come to a point of birth where you go from relative to the non-relative and then you go back. As I said in the morning, I can always show you the non-identified absence but you come back to presence – and both is not it. I can talk you to death and by talking you to death, there's an absence of 'me'. But where there can be an absence of 'me' there can be a resurrection of the 'me' – sooner or later. Because that what could be talked to death, can resurrect again – naturally. But it is possible to talk it to death – leading you to a point where this mind cannot breath anymore. Where you have to be what-you-are, but it will always come back.

So, you have to be what-you-are in both. In that absence and in the presence of 'me' you have to be what-you-cannot-not-be. Because what-you-cannot-not-be is in the presence of the 'me' and in the absence of the 'me' – what-it-is. So, there's a difference. There's resistance which is mind and there's no-resistance which is no-mind. But both are always shifting from there to there. They can only shift because there is one who is realizing this shift.

Q: But when you say the identified and non-identified both are not it, you cannot get a picture of what-it-is. You can only say it is not...

K: I can only tell you what it is not.

Q: In religion, for God they made a painting which has a triangle and an eye inside it...

K: The eye of God. The perception has to be there so that all of that can happen. The triangle and the eye, that's the symbol for perception – but there's no perceiver. As you said yesterday the apperception, the perception without the perceiver. The perception in which the perceiver appears and disappears in. The perception never appears and never disappears.

The perception with an image of perceiver, of perception, it's perceiving a presence. The perception in which there is no-perceiver and nothing to perceive, there is the absence. Both are dream realization. So, realizing is presence and non-realizing is absence. The perception is always awake – never asleep. The eye of God never sleeps.

Q: And does the triangle means the father, the son and the holy ghost?

K: Doesn't matter. Who cares?

Q: What about the original sin?

K: That's you – that's your spiritual name. [Laughter] The original sin is that God woke up and fell in love with himself and now you are the result of God falling in love with its image. You are the result of God being in love with himself. You are the result of the original sin. You have no business in it, it's all God's business. It's his-story not your story. The narcissistic God! And you are a result of the narcissistic love.

Q: There are some deadly sins in Christianity that cannot be forgotten. For that you have to burn in hell forever...

K: So, what sin did you commit that you are in hell now? The deadly sin is – you believe that you are born because that makes you a mortal. So, you are already dead – that's a deadly sin. That puts you into the hell of fear and all what comes with the body.

Q: You talk a lot about hell. Do you have an imagination about heaven?

K: The oneness – non-identification. That's heaven, staying in the 'I Amness', being non-identified with everything.

Q: But that's also temporary...

K: I never said that's final, I just say that's heaven.

Q: So, hell also must be temporary...

K: No! Because heaven is part of the hell. There's heaven and hell – but only in hell. [Laughing]

Q: Because both are in time?

K: No. Both are the ways you realize yourself – in comfort and discomfort. Discomfort would be hell and comfort would be heaven. Discomfort is being identified and comfort is being non-identified. Both are the ways you realize yourself. Both are infinite.

Q: But I always thought that the real is infinite but the realization is temporary?

K: You think? How many times did you listen to me? That's why I say, I spit in bullshit because no one listens to what I say. How many times did I say that the real and realization in nature are not different and both are infinite? What are you sitting here for?

Q: Both are infinite?

K: There are no both, they are not different in nature. Who wants to have my job? Now you made it really bad. I just pee in the air.

Q: I can't hear it enough...

K: You can never hear it enough, you resist.

Q: Maybe I have a little Alzheimer...

K: I hope. Maybe you forget to come. [Laughter] Sounds promising. Maybe you forget Christa, then there's no problem anymore.

Q [Another visitor]: So, this entire... is nothing but you fucking yourself? It doesn't need a thought to exist, it doesn't need a word to exist...

K: It just fucks itself. In India the *lingam* is the first Adam – the light of awareness and the mother is the space. Then the light starts to vibrate with the question – Why? The why-bration in the space creates the whole manifestation. And all what you can experience is the answer of the question – Why? I Am What?

Then comes the infinite answer of the infinite manifestation – Boom! – That! But you always think that you need to see the whole puzzle but you can only see aspects of the puzzle. You will never see the whole. You want to step back to see the total picture but you will not. Being the whole picture is easy – just the puzzler is part of the puzzle – that's all. Then it is complete because the puzzler is part of the puzzle. There is a completeness – instantly.

It was always there, but you wanted to be apart from the puzzle. Then you are always puzzled that one thing is always missing – 'You'. You were always there, but by you wanting to be a separate God, apart God, who wants to be 'special' – a puzzler who wants to see the complete picture, that puzzles you infinitely. There's always a frustration inside because you try your best and it never works.

You can have a holistic point of view, all of that, all the religions – and nothing works. When you are just that – the puzzler is not different from the puzzle – instantly you are That what you cannot not be. It was always fulfillment – peace. But not as one apart from it – never. For me it's the most fitting picture – you are the fucker, the fucking and the fucked, and that's – fucked!

February 12, 2012. Evening Talk.
Thailand

Even saying that there is nothing to find, is a goal on the way

K: [Joking with a French lady] She wanted to look for what is good about French and she found only bad things.

Q: Madam Curie found out something...

K: That was worse. She found out that she was dying by what she found out. It's stupid to find something that kills you. [Laughter] That's what you find out. It will kill you. The moment you come to whatever you're looking for, it kills you right away. So, it's stupid to look for it. By accident you find it and then it kills you – shit! Scientifically proven dead.

You really look for something where you cannot exist. It's crazy! So, permanently you have a suicide intention and you're looking for something what may kill you. Because you don't even like to exist. And then you say, 'Oh, I'm so much in love'. No one loves anything. Everyone hates every moment that he exists. [Laughter]

It will strike you whether you like it or not. God will cut you down in one [making a lightening sound] and not hesitate to get rid of a little piece of meat. How many wars did we have? Consciousness sending meats to war just so that they meet their final destination – Pang! – Pieces of flesh flying all over the world. That's called black *tantra*.

Q [Another visitor]: It's weird that we're looking for a way to kill the 'me'...

K: No. It's not weird, it's natural. Because any moment you exist, you experience misery and you want to end misery. So, it's natural that you want to end it.

Q: But we're not going to be able to...

K: Of course you will end. You came and you will be gone. You don't even have to do something for it, it happens by itself. You came by itself and you will be gone by itself. So, what do you worry about?

Q: When the body dies...

K: There's nothing that dies. Nothing is born and nothing will die. So, what's your problem? Nothing happens. So, you wait for nothing because nothing will happen. Because nothing happened when you were born and nothing will happen when you die. So, what are you waiting for? You don't even know what are you waiting for. But for that, you're waiting and that's called ignorance.

Q: I'm waiting for the ego to disappear...

K: Yeah. The ego waits for the ego to disappear – forever.

Q: Or the 'me'...

K: You see, that's suicide. You're dreaming about not being. You're believing in a dream. You really believe that you can really get rid of 'you'. You really have a hope of a way out. Keep dreaming baby. That makes you a baby who's born, dreaming of being born and dreaming of being dead. The entire dream came true. The dream became the truth and now you're trapped into that. And still nothing happens. So, what to do? Love kills. Out of love you're here and because you're here, you're dead. [Laughing]

Being in love with a bloody idea kills you. So, love kills – and you cannot help it. You always fall in love again with that shit. Then that shit is dead, you don't want to be the shit. But then it's too late.

Poor you! Being born in a piece of shit and by now wanting to get out of it you confirm that you're in this shit. That makes you feel shitty. Isn't it a joke?

Q [Another visitor]: When you tell it, it is...

K: When I say, it becomes a joke but when you say does it become serious? [Laughing] I just point to the helplessness, to the carefree. After the helplessness comes the carefree.

Q: This thing that is waiting for something to happen, waiting for enlightenment...

K: It's not waiting, it permanently tries to kill itself. You even try to kill time.

Q: Is it the concept 'I' that's waiting or is it something else?

K: Out of love for yourself you want to end misery – moment by moment. And because you want to end misery, you're miserable. What else? Out of love for what-you-are, you want to end that discomfort and because you want to end discomfort, you want to end yourself and by that you suffer. By trying to end yourself. Isn't it crazy? Totally crazy.

You want to end the discomfort, but that's what-you-are. You can only experience yourself in discomfort. So, any moment you want to end this discomfort, you want to end yourself and by that you suffer. Isn't that crazy? You want to avoid yourself. If that's not crazy and stupid, what else is? That's the only ignorance which is there – that you think that you can end yourself.

You have to realize yourself and you have to realize yourself in discomfort – in ignorance. And I sit here and say, be happy that it's ignorance and not truth that you experience. But you're unhappy because you want to make it true or you want to end it. You want to love it, embrace it or by the wisdom of emptiness, destroy it. Both is trying to control it – and by both of that you suffocate. Isn't it crazy?

I sit here just to point to the craziness of you trying to strangle yourself. Even by trying to open up, you strangle yourself. Making yourself bigger – you strangle yourself. Making yourself smaller – you strangle yourself. Both come out of a belief system that something has to happen – for 'me'.

[Mocking] I have to be 'bigger', I want to embrace everything. I have to know that I'm everything and if I cannot do that, I will be nothing. I'll go to the nothingness. Then you're pissed. If I cannot embrace everything, the bliss of being everything, in the love of being everything, then I fuck it all and I go to the nothingness. Then I just forget myself. If I cannot be pleased by myself that way, I go away – totally. I get pissed-off totally – fuck it all. ME! [Laughing]

I always find jokes everywhere and the biggest joke is you suffer about yourself and only because you want to end yourself. Because you want to make yourself infinite, you suffer. Because even by trying to make yourself infinite, you confirm that there's one who needs it. Even that is suffering, suffocating. It's crazy!

Q [Another visitor]: So, this is all in the nature of the consciousness that you suffer and there's nothing that can change it?

K: I don't know if it's in the nature, but it behaves like that. I don't say, it has to be like this. I just say it's stupid. Then you expect something from that bullshit, stupid consciousness for yourself that it can deliver something to you that you're looking for. So, what to do? You cannot trust yourself – you know that. Never! The Self is always stupid. You have to be inspite that stupid Self – what-you-are.

The Self is always stupid because the Self is already a lover and out of love for himself, it wants to end whatever is there. *Shiva* knowing *Shiva*, when there is a *Shiva*, it wants to destroy everything, whatever can be destroyed – even himself. But he cannot. He always tries, but he'll never succeed. Crazy! So, even *Shiva* is crazy! *Shiva* knowing *Shiva* is totally crazy and stupid. That you really didn't expect.

Even *Shiva* is a bloody husband who believes in love and jealousy and all those stories, chopping the head of his son. Then you pray to that impotent guy. So, if there would be a *Shiva*, he should strike me now. You always fear fairy tales. [Mocking] Then you may still say that *Shiva* struck her and grace came from behind and struck my brain and there was a flash going through my system. – Pang! – Struck down by grace! You can make a story out of everything. Then you write it down and make a book. The day I was struck by *Shiva* and then the others say – Me too. [Laughter]

I don't even have to please *Shiva* because I Am That which is prior and beyond of any *Shiva*. You can call that as nature of *Shiva*. But how can the nature of *Shiva* be afraid of an image of *Shiva*?

Q [Another visitor]: It's like fighting against your shadow...

K: You think that your shadow can kill you – what an idea! But you're so afraid of your shadow. It's everywhere, wherever you go. Only at night in the darkness of the darkness, there is no shadow. [Laughter] Then you can rest that there's no shadow. And then every morning the awareness wakes up and then – shadow. [Jokingly whining] And then you want to bury your shadow because you're so fucking afraid about your shadow.

There's a famous story which says meditation is like digging your grave because you want to bury your shadow. All your tendencies, all your shadows, all what you're afraid of, you bury in some grave – and you dig it as deep as you can. Then you want to see all your tendencies, all your fears down in the grave. Then you close the grave as fast as you can and then you say – Yes I made it! I worked it all out! Now they are really gone. You don't even dare to open your eyes anymore. Then you run around and say – as I don't see my shadow, I don't have a shadow.

But then by whatever curiosity you open your eyes and then all the shadows are back and all the tendencies and all the fears on top of the grave. The tombstone waits for you. It was so nice without the shadow. I like these stories.

Q [Another visitor]: We're all stories...

K: Yeah. The stupidity of imagining that you can get rid of your shadow. Reality will always realize itself as a shadow of itself. It can never realize itself as what-it-is. So, it has to realize itself as a shadow of itself. The first shadow is 'I' – the light of *Shiva* – it's a shadow of light. Already the light of *Shiva* is the shadow of the light. The experience of awareness is already the shadow of That – is light and light will never know itself in its nature. The first shadow – is light, the experience of light. The next is space – absence. Then the next is all what comes out of that – shadow land and then you're afraid of it.

Q: It's amazing...

K: Yeah. You're amazed about yourself. You're amazed how stupid can one be! What a perfect trap is in front of you. What a perfect shadow land! What a perfect absolute trap is waiting for you every morning and you cannot avoid to fall into that trap. You cannot not wake up. When you wake up, the trap waits for you.

Q: So, this thought of needing to be conscious...

K: Is another trap.

Q: So, waking up in the morning is just helplessness...

K: There's nothing to do anymore, it's too late. Whatever you do after being awake, is try to end misery, try to end your shadow – and you will never end your shadow. You always try to kill the phantom but the phantom cannot be killed because the phantom is a realization of what is not a phantom.

What-you-are can only realize itself as a phantom – and it will never end. As that what is realizing itself does not start and never ends, the phantom never starts and never ends. So what do you want to end? By trying to end the phantom, you try to end yourself and then you suffer that you don't want to exist. How stupid can it get?

Q: It's impossible for the phantom to...

K: The phantom never had any choice.

Q: But is it possible for the phantom to stop thinking of the solutions?

K: The phantom was never thinking, that's the problem.

Q: So, consciousness is forever...

K: Stupid!

Q: Making adjustments...

K: Stupid! Just call it stupid. Trying to adjust something what never needs to be adjusted is stupid. Trying to create a harmony which was never lost. There is only harmony because there's no two. There's an absolute harmony, there's no two. It's an idea that there's a second self, that you and your shadow is different – then there's two, one who has a shadow. Then there's two and that's already bullshit. [Laughter]

In German we say, don't be a shadow of yourself. So, be the shadow not knowing the shadow. Be the light not knowing the light – absolutely not knowing what-you-are and what-you-are-not. That is what-you-cannot-not-be. But any moment you imagine, to be that light which has a shadow, it's already separation of a dream. The dream is that you are separate from what-you-are or there is something else as 'you'. That's called misery.

Q [Another visitor]: Are there two shadows?

K: No. The light is already a shadow. Whatever you understand after that, is another fleeting understanding of a fleeting shadow that understands that there are two shadows. It's crazy! No way out!

When I say – you have to be inspite of your understanding and stupidity and bloody love affair with yourself, because already that is stupidity, being in love with yourself. Even the idea of love is already stupid, but what can you do? Trying to end it or change it is as stupid as not changing it.

Just be absolute what-you-are and as absolute as you-are, as absolute stupid you-are. Just be as you are – absolute. Then you're absolute knowledge, you're absolute absence of any idea of what-you-are. When you experience yourself, you're absolute stupid and you can only experience yourself in absolute stupidity. Any so-called insight or conclusion is as stupid as the biggest joke on the earth. So, what to do? Never ending misery. [Laughing]

You have to experience yourself as a devil. The moment the devil is there, there's hell. There's no devil without hell and only in hell, there's an idea of heaven and hell and oneness and all you can come up with. All the shadows and the things are there, because you are there! The moment you experience yourself, you're That what is the devil and out of That experiencer, you create your own bloody hell. Hell-elujah! [Laughter]

Without the presence of That what you imagine to be, there would not be any possibility of any second imagination. The devil is a Diabolo – lives from idea of two. He needs two. He will always make sure that there's two, even if that means he's in hell. If it means that there's hell, he's okay with it, because he needs it. What would he do without hell? And the hell can only remain stable because there's an idea of heaven. Only in hell there is a hope, the hell will be there forever. All the religions and all the Popes are there so that the hell continues. All the teachers and all the *gurus* are there because the devil is there.

In India, they even say that the guru is the devil – the teacher, who keeps the hell alive. He's Lucifer, the bringer of light, the promise of enlightenment. Who promises you enlightenment? Only the one who believes that light needs light – that you need to be enlightened – that he got the light. Yes, he [devil] wants the light and he needs the light. Because without the presence, he cannot exist. He really believes in it and he sometimes believes, that he can give you something and you need it! So, you cannot even blame him.

All the so-called *gurus* and teachers, they talk about something that they really believe in. It's not like they want to cheat you. They really are honest, that's really the problem. You cannot even beat them up for what they say because they really believe in it. They're core-splitting honest. It even works! That's the worst that it even works! That there is some advantage in the 'now'. That is because it works it's so much hell and only in hell you have to work. Only in hell you need something to work. So, hell of a work in health kitchen. You have a recipe of a peace of cake!

What am I doing here? I'm not here to spoil the fun. I'm here to tell the devil that you can stay here for ever, no one cares. Amazingly, if he really sees that you don't really need to fight that the hell will be there, he can even rest in hell. There's peace in hell. So, Karl can do whatever. So, even Karl can rest in that – that no one wants him to go – not even Karl wants Karl to go. No need for anything.

So, out of a relative Karl, he became an absolute Karl, just by being what one is. Amazing! And that you cannot call it love, it even kills Karl – just this little agreement. Karl can stay as long as Karl is there. If Karl is gone, not even Karl cares. I have no contradiction with myself. There's no fight. There's no two – Karl and what I Am are not different. So, how can I have a fight with what I Am? How can I suffer about what I Am? Come on!

There's no need of pleasing myself and I don't need to be pleased by whatever this is. So, what to do? As this cannot be pleased and I cannot please myself, no one has to please me and I don't have to please anyone. That's more than pleasing and you're quite pleased that no one, not even yourself wants to please you. You rest in that – whatever. It's a fulfillment that you don't need to be fulfilled. There's a sweetness that you don't have to taste the sweetness – of any bullshit open heart or anything or that someone loves you. Who gives a fuck about it? Even if you love yourself or not, there's an absolute carefreeness. This bloody idea of love drops as soon as it pops up.

Q [Another visitor]: Protecting an image...

K: There's no protection of an image. Now you start again – your little war. Now you start again to fight for yourself – protecting an image. Who needs to protect a bloody image? To excuse oneself of what one has not done is stupid as hell too. You're not in a court case and you're not a judge for yourself. And you don't have to justify what you've not done. Come on!

All this bloody justification and trying to be in love with what you have done or not done, and always justifying that bullshit story of Martin and how Martin is? What has Martin done or not done? What did Martin achieve in his life? How many enlightened backgrounds did he go to? Does it have any relevance? All that fucking bullshit.

You're not even irrelevant. If you would be irrelevant, you still would be. You're neither relevant or irrelevant. If you see I cannot be relevant, you go to the irrelevant – I'm nothing. You can still survive as a phantom, as being nothing. So, you think if I cannot be that relevant *avatar* controlling the whole universe, than I will be irrelevant – nothing. If I cannot be this, I can survive as that. It's just a shift to another phantom state. It's always tricky.

I'm sitting here pointing how tricky you are. You don't have to be tricky to survive. There's no need for survival because you are not born. Whatever is born is already dead. So, even that doesn't need to fight for survival because that what's already dead, is already dead. How can you call an image alive? How can you call a phenomenal experience – life?

But you do that. You call That, as being born and being alive. Come on! Even to recognize that it's a fleeting shadow, only a shadow needs to recognize that it's a fleeting shadow. For what-you-are, you don't even need to recognize that it's a fleeting shadow. You just shift from one ignorance to another ignorance. From relative to absolute ignorance. Wisdom is as ignorant as no-wisdom. You're doomed anyway – wis-dumb. So, have another sip of coffee!

Q [Another visitor]: Absolute ignorance?

K: Doesn't know any ignorance, as absolute knowledge doesn't know any knowledge, but the moment you know one of it, there's relative ignorance and relative knowledge. Relative knowledge and relative ignorance – is misery. You know that.

So, know yourself as you know yourself in deep-deep sleep. The knowledge of what-you-are, you cannot lose and you cannot gain. So, inspite of all the shadow experiences, all what you can call whatever experience, not because. So, being absolute ignorance is not knowing any ignorance. For sure there's no one who's ignorant in ignorance. If there's one who's ignorant in ignorance – that's relative ignorance.

When you are ignorant, you don't even know what is ignorance and what's not-ignorance. So, not knowing ignorance or not-ignorance is the nature of knowledge – and ignorance. That's the nature of nature. That what never knows anything about nature of what-is and what-is-not nature. So, the absolute presence of one who knows or doesn't – That is what-you-are. That, you are, every night and now you try to...

Q: Make some noise...

K: You want to end disturbance – that's all, but by trying to end disturbance, you create one who's disturbed. What an idea! You cannot otherwise, without disturbance, experience yourself. I agree – the dream about yourself is disturbance. In absolute comfort of your experience, there's a disturbance, but That is what-you-are. So, you experience disturbance but there's no one who is disturbed.

Only by trying to end disturbance, you create permanently a 'one' who is disturbed – suffering about the presence, trying to end the presence, trying to end yourself. Or even trying not to end yourself, whatever you do then, is what? But what to do – shit happens. So, if I call it – shit happens – I mean it. You cannot even stop that – trying to end something. You are totally fucked! For now and forever.

Q [Another visitor]: It's really bad...

K: It's not so bad – it's worse! You cannot imagine how bad that is.

Q [Another visitor]: You try everything to avoid that...

K: You try to avoid the avoider.

Q [Another visitor]: Is it the idea of surviving?

K: You just want comfort – permanently in whatever you do. Whatever you try to do, you try to end discomfort. If that means you should kill yourself, you would kill yourself for it – if you could and you try. But you cannot. You can never kill yourself and you can never get away from what-you-are. So what? But you try. By that trying, seeking, you are love-sick. Then you want to be healed, but the moment you want to be healed, you want to understand, you confirm one who is ignorant. It's a total absolute trap for yourself.

How can you escape that trap which is made by what-you-are? Only you can cheat yourself so very well and so deeply and only you can punish yourself, so very profoundly as no one else can punish you – as there's no other anyway. It's stupid, but what can you do? I have no idea, but having no idea is having too many ideas already. So, even that is stupid – having no idea. What to do?

Even looking stupid doesn't help. [Laughter]

Q [Another visitor]: So, that's the big *koan*, the origin of all the *koans*...

K: You want to understand yourself – and you cannot. It's the absolute *koan* – That what is knowledge will never know the knowledge, but you try and you try to break it. By being concentrated on that absolute *koan* – trying to know yourself – is *jñana* yoga. By being concentrated, that nothing else matters anymore, whatever 'else' drops away. Just by being absolutely concentrated on that *koan* – yourself. The phantom cannot remain in That. Sooner or later, it breaks down because there's nothing to breathe anymore. No relative knowledge, nothing, because you're only concentrated on That what-you-are. And if that has to happen, it will happen.

So, if the Self is really after the Self, it will kill the Self – just by being that. The idea of Self cannot remain. God totally and absolutely concentrates on himself, on That what is God. The idea of God would cease away, just by That. That's called the rising of the inner sun and by that inner sun, of absolute knowledge, all that what you can imagine ceases away like butter in the sun.

You cannot even avoid rising of the inner sun – the darkness, the mystery of what-you-are. It will even chase the relative light away. If *Shiva* wants to destroy the idea of *Shiva*, it will destroy it when it destroys it and not one second before. And whatever the shadow has done before – it was just a joke. And with That – what is the sun – all those *vipasanna* techniques and all the meditation and all what you have done, is just peeing in the wind. [Laughter]

The sailor needs to know in which side to pee. That's the most important rule for a sailor. That's why you hold your finger in the air to find out where does the wind come from so that you don't pee into the wind or you don't vomit into the wind – for sure not. [Laughter]

But that is what the seeker is doing – always vomiting into the wind – and then all that vomit comes back to him.

Q [Another visitor]: I got something... [Laughter]

K: I got something out of it. [Laughter] That's called pee with the wind, not go with the flow. [Laughter] Wherever the wind blows. Osho says go with the flow but Karl says pee with the wind and don't try to sail against the wind because that's really stupid. But if you want to sail against the wind, you're like Martin [referring to a visitor]. He always sails against the wind and then he complains that he's tired and he's always stuck.

Q [Another visitor]: What do you mean by 'concentrated'...

K: When awareness puts awareness to awareness, awareness can't do it by itself. It will happen – by itself. By itself and not by any outside event or anything what will happen. It happens by itself – by awareness itself, which is awareness, but not by any 'one' who is aware or not aware – asshole.

Q: Just to make sure... [Laughter]

K: So, it's always inspite – never because of whatever happens in the dream, whatever you've done, where you're born, where your parents are, which lineage you come from, who your master was – and all of that. All of that is what? Peeing in the wind. Walking the line of a prostitute – having a lineage and following it.

When I say I'm always saved by my laziness – I mean it. And for me, even trying to be lazy is too much work. So when people ask me why are you still sitting and talking and traveling so much? I would say not trying to do it is more work and more doing than just letting it happen, as it happens anyway. So, the laziness of what I Am is uninterrupted. What I Am has never done anything. And the rest is automatic unfolding of – shit. The next shit is as much shit and shitty as the one before.

Wherever I Am – it's bad. So what? There's no end of the I Am and there's no beginning of the I Am. Even the I Am never starts and never ends and wherever I Am – it's bad. So what? Whenever there's I Am, there's discomfort – already. And you cannot get rid of the I Am. That's why – Am I - I Am – so what?

Q: Too lazy to be lazy...

K: Yeah. The laziness doesn't have to be lazy. And that what needs to be lazy, to be lazy, is trying to pee in the wind again. He wants to piss-off, but wherever he pees, there's wind blowing against him. But for absolute what-you-are, the wind always blows with you, the whole energy is always blowing your way. Because you are That what is creating the wind, and you're the blowing. And you're the blower, the blowing and what can be blown. That is being with the wind.

THE SONG OF IRRELEVANCE

But the moment you want to go against it, you go against the wind, you go against yourself. So, you're peeing against yourself, you vomit against yourself and then you complain that you stink.

Q: And when there's no wind, I'm spontaneous...

K: Then you do things by in-stinkt – stinker. In India there was a guy called Yogi Changdev who lived for fourteen hundred years and moved the mountains and he was very proud that he had so much power and energy. Then he came to a Jñaneshwara [13th Century, Maharashtra, India] who was sitting on the wall and told him – Look what I can do. The guy was sitting on the wall and suddenly the wall moved forward with Jñaneshwara towards Changdev without any effort and Changdev was shocked.

All his so-called powers, *siddhis* and energies were just a joke in the wind by one lazy guy sitting on the wall. The whole wall just worked for him without any effort. The whole universe without any effort was doing what had to be done. All the bloody *avatars*, *siddhis* were just a joke – peeing in the wind. All that effort, surviving fourteen hundred years and counting every fucking second – because all of that is misery. Fourteen hundred years of misery against one guy who's sitting on the wall. Come on!

Q: So in a way that effort is attached and assured to someone...

K: The effort is just reactions, reactions, reactions. There's not even one who makes an effort. There's just reaction of a reaction of a reaction of your grand, grand, grandfathers or mothers. Bloody ancestors now having an erection. It's not even your erection – imagine! It's your grandfather's erection, because maybe he had a Viagra hundred years ago and now it comes up [Laughter] and you wonder what happened now? It was so quiet for a long time and now my grandfather comes again!

Q: You mean there's hope!

K: There's no hope. There was no viagra hundred years ago. It's crazy! There's a reaction to an outside event and you don't even know why you react, but then you make it a story and then you fish into your grandfather's, ancestors to find out where does that come from? Am I German? Do Germans react like that?

Q: Such a headache for such a short period of time...

K: Whatever has a head should ache. It's the nature of a head to ache. So, there's more or less ache. What to do?

Q [Another visitor]: When you say that, I try to avoid the avoider...

K: When the avoider tries to avoid to avoid – it's a joke. The avoider tries to avoid the avoider.

Q [Another visitor]: There's so much effort in being a shadow...

K: Now you claim that you make an effort. That you can get tired. That's the 'poor me' state. [Mocking] I'm a poor steak, what can I do? I don't want to be a steak. I miss myself in the steak so much. It's a me-steak. Help me! Pitiful. What a pity!

Q [Another visitor]: Sadness is okay but pitying the one who's the sad one is...

K: Being sad is already quite pitiful.

Q: But pitying the sadness...

K: It's already too late. That's what you have to do. By pitying you just make it worse, but it's already bad. So, why not? It's not so bad, but it's worse.

Q: And the so-called joy is forgetting that...

K: Now you make it a technique again.

Q: That's right...

K: It doesn't work baby. Who has to forget, baby? What baby needs to forget to be a baby? You just drop one concept and pick up another one. You always try all the possibilities and nothing works. And that's your job. Trying all possible ways and no way

The Song of Irrelevance

delivers. So what did Buddha say? The way is the goal. And what does that mean?

Q: There's nothing to become...

K: That's just another idea. Even 'nothing to find' is a goal on the way. Being the way not knowing the way. So, you are the goal means you are the way. You cannot not be the way and there's an infinite way. By not knowing any way, being the way, there's no way. It does not have a conclusion.

Q: So, being what is that which cannot be done...

K: What-you-cannot-not-be. Just stay where you-cannot-not-be and not make it a bloody circle. Don't try to get behind yourself or in front of yourself. Just be what-you-cannot-not-be. But what you try to do is, you always try to circle yourself. You want to go around yourself, you want to know yourself. For that you have to go out of yourself. By that you become an image – a phantom. Like a satellite around That what is the *sat*. So, you become a satellite turning around yourself. Then you complain that you're out of orbit or you're in orbit.

Everyone works for that next word. The living words find their own way, you don't have to work for it. That's called living words – not trying to fix something or making it as an interesting statement. For me talking bullshit is as good as not talking bullshit. The words will find themselves to whatever interesting new whatever. It's always unique and new and always living and changing the form. Sometimes they make sense, sometimes not but no one cares. They're sense-free.

For sure – thank God there's no meaning in it. How much bullshit can I talk? Infinite bullshit. And who cares? No one.

Q [Another visitor]: It appears as if totality of consciousness sometimes has a memory...

K: Sometimes? It's not sometimes, it's now, here...

Q: Sometimes it's your grandfather...

K: They are all here-now.

Q: And there's nothing to memorize because they're all here?

K: It's never-never. It's the one hand clapping again. [Hitting his hand on the head] It's me, it's me, it's me. That's the mind always trying to clear the fallen leaves and what do these bloody trees do? Create more leaves so that you may clean the forest again. That's trying to clean up – just to make it clear. It's always unique, all the leaves from today and not yesterday or from last season. You always want to clean up leaves from this season.

Q: To avoid any misunderstanding...

K: Yeah. Just for once and for all, you want to make it clear. [Laughter] Then you turn around and see another leaf – another be-leaf [belief] system – Oh, I just want to make it clear. I want to get rid of the be-leaf system that it's clear. Then I believe that without believing that I'm clear of believing – then it's clear.

Q [Another visitor]: When you talked about UG [Krishnamurti] and clearing of all the information system...

K: No. That's not what I meant, it's not clearing out.

Q: In the so-called calamity, the burning out of information in the oneness...

K: It's burning out that one who could have a memory. It goes directly to That owner – burning down the house. The first card of the card house gets burnt down and without the first card, there was never any house. The first believer gets burnt down – directly. By the rising of the inner sun, the light gets burnt out right away. The imaginary light of awareness gets burnt out – just by That light you-are.

So, it never goes for little cleaning up of the forest.

Q: It's not like burning out of this one [pointing to his body]...

K: But it all depends on that one. Without Martin, there would be no universe, there would not even be sun. There would be no belief system without the believer. The very first and imaginary experience of the believer gets burnt out – by itself. That is Ramana's awareness of awareness. The awareness gives awareness to awareness – by being awareness. And there is no one who is or is-not aware in That. That doesn't even know awareness.

So, it kills the very first imaginary awareness – which is already imaginary awareness, the experience of awareness – by being That which never needs any experience of awareness and no one can do that, and no one has to do that. Whatever you try, keeps the awareness alive – this imaginary one. So, what to do? That will never end and being what-you-cannot-not-be is still what-it-is – that's always carefree and the caretaker in front of it, will always take care. The caretaker called consciousness will always care about itself. So, you better be inspite of that what-you-are – always inspite – with and without – that's all.

But Martin can only be 'with', Martin cannot be 'without'. So, Martin is called the shadow. That fleeting leaf, that fleeting shadow, which came and will be gone and then there maybe another shadow – who cares? What-you-are never cared about the presence of Martin, I tell you. That's called acceptance – not even knowing Martin – not even knowing itself. So, what are you waiting for?

To wait for That which never knows itself and by knowing yourself kill yourself? It really gives a shit if you're there or not. Do you really think that absolute existence really needs you to go to be what-it-is? How much arrogance can be there? And this arrogance has to be punished by suffering – instantly. This little French inside needs to be punished.

And you always feed your own hell – you know that. You put more belief system in the fire of hell. And there will never be no belief system left, you're sure about that. There will always be enough belief system for you to burn as a devil in hell – burning and burning and burning – longing and longing for what-you-are. The longing will never stop for Martin.

And that what is Martin cannot long for itself because there is no Martin who can long and needs to long and there's no bridge between that. That what you call Martin will always have a different realm – that's called consciousness, awareness – whatever you call something, whatever you name – will always long for that absence of that what is longing. And that's a never ending story of the longing consciousness longing to know consciousness or the absence of consciousness.

You have to be inspite of that misery of Martin – which always has different names. Earlier it was the misery of Jesus, misery of whoever was before you, misery of all your ancestors and the misery of all those who will follow – will be the experience of the misery of Martin.

Q [Another visitor, joking]: Thank you Martin for taking all that...

K: But you can even call it Paulo's. Since he was thanking you, now we call it Paulo – very low, the little Diabolo – Paulo. [Laughter]

That's what I'm telling you, you cannot avoid discomfort. The discomfort of now – is Martin and after Martin there will be another experience of discomfort and the next discomfort and the next discomfort and the next discomfort. You will not find comfort in any experience. Whatever you can find is discomfort – the discomfort of separation – which is the very nature of experience. It needs separation, without separation – no experience. So, what to do?

And you can always call it different. A different Martin. Seven billion different discomforts now running on this earth. Waking up every morning in the discomfort of personal and impersonal ideas having a dependency of body-mind tra...la...la... So what to do?

Do you really believe that when Martin is not there, this will end? When this peace of meat – Martin – is gone? When this me-steak Martin is gone, there will be another me-steak – steak after steak – in the butchery of life. What a slaughter house! And you still think that you can slaughter that which was never there?

Q: Steak in, steak out...

K: Is something at stake, Martin? You're in a barbecue of life here – me and you on a barbecue. Let's have a drink together. Baking me and baking you, you become a bakery man. Then you think that the bakery man doesn't go into the oven anymore. So, the bakery man becomes the devil, putting Martin in the hell.

February 27, 2012. Morning Talk.
Thailand

www.ingramcontent.com/pod-product-compliance
Lightning Source LLC
Chambersburg PA
CBHW070647160426
43194CB00009B/1613